A 60-Day Journal
Challenge

Ask
Yourself
This

Ultimate Life
Lessons From And For
My Girlfriends

A 60-Day Journal
Challenge

*Ask Yourself This*

Ultimate Life
Lessons From And For
My Girlfriends

Shari Leid

Capucia LLC
211 Pauline Drive #513
York, PA 17402
www.capuciapublishing.com
Send questions to: support@capuciapublishing.com

Paperback ISBN: 978-1-954920-40-8
eBook ISBN: 978-1-954920-41-5
Library of Congress Control Number: 2022916487

*Cover Design: Ranilo Cabo*
*Layout: Ranilo Cabo*
*All author photos: Wendy K. Yalom/www.Wendykyalom.com*
*Photos of author's friends: Natalie Wallace/www.nataliewallacephotography.com*
*Editor and Proofreader: Janis Hunt Johnson/www.askjanis.com*
*Book Midwife: Carrie Jareed*

Printed in the United States of America

Capucia LLC is proud to be a part of the Tree Neutral® program. Tree Neutral offsets the number of trees consumed in the production and printing of this book by taking proactive steps such as planting trees in direct proportion to the number of trees used to print books. To learn more about Tree Neutral, please visit treeneutral.com.

*I dedicate this final book in the* Friendship *series in memory of my dad who taught me the value of friendships through the way he lived—valuing the relationships he cultivated with his colleagues, students, friends, and family members.*

# Preface

The journey of the *Friendship* series began in December of 2019. I turned forty-nine years old that month, and leading up to my fiftieth birthday, I challenged myself to meet with fifty women in my life over the course of the year — some old friends, some more recent acquaintances — to let each of them know what I've learned from them. I embarked on this project with the belief that everyone we meet is both our teacher and our student. This personal experiment became so impactful in my life and in the lives of the women I met with, that I created a movement: the #5050friendshipflowchallenge — which is highlighted in what became the first book of the *Friendship* series, *The 50/50 Friendship Flow: Life Lessons From And For My Girlfriends.*

I did not plan to write a second book, but then the pandemic hit, and stay-at-home orders were issued in my state. During this time, I took a MasterClass® course taught by television broadcaster Robin Roberts on the topic of effective and authentic communication. Ms. Roberts shared that her mom taught her to make her mess her message. Her words resonated with me and prompted me to continue what I had begun the year before — one-on-one dates with girlfriends, but this time via Zoom — to ask, "What is the mess that became your message?" From this experience, the second book was born, *Make Your Mess Your Message: More Life Lessons From And For My Girlfriends.*

I now had a series on my hands, which has led me to this very book — *Ask Yourself This: Ultimate Life Lessons From And For My Girlfriends.* In this final volume of the *Friendship* series, I asked my girlfriends things which at first glance were just basic life questions; but as the answers unfolded, I found that these simple questions led to the most amazing conversations. In addition to the subject inquiry, I began each conversation by learning where my girlfriend was born and ending the conversation by asking her what she would like to have written on her headstone. These conversations not only sparked a moment of self-reflection for my girlfriends, but also prompted me to ask the same questions of myself — leading to a year-long journey of self-coaching and self-discovery.

The *Friendship* series has been a labor of love for my girlfriends, fueling my life purpose to support and elevate women, with gratitude for the imperfectly perfect life that I've been gifted. During each meeting, I explained that I was writing about the thoughts and experiences shared with me by my girlfriends because I strongly believe that each story I share will be meaningful to another woman — a woman who will pick up the book and need to hear that story, that chapter, that life mess, that reflection and lesson, on that day. Each chapter is written for just that one reader, to change her life by changing her mindset. I don't know who she is — it may be *you*.

Each time I completed the writing of a chapter, I closed my eyes and said a prayer of gratitude for my girlfriend who had allowed herself to be vulnerable by sharing her story. I said a prayer of hope and love for the woman her story touches. Yes, I sent a prayer into the universe for you.

This book is written for you to journal through each day for sixty days straight. Did you know it takes roughly sixty days to form a habit? Using this book as a tool to form a journaling habit — which is the best free tool for self-coaching — will give you a better understanding of who you are. It will help bring some of your unconscious beliefs to the surface so that you can reflect and consider whether they are serving you, and see if you need to rewrite any of those beliefs to support your goals. The process will also remind you that you have all of the skills, tools, and talents to manifest and create the life of your dreams.

#60dayjournalchallenge

# Contents

## Ask Yourself This — *Early Adult Years*

# Foreword

Imet Shari several years ago in the way many of her friends have met her: through an informal social gathering of women, organized by her. The event was a moms' night out. Our college-aged children were just grade-schoolers at the time. A mutual friend invited me, explaining that Shari loved meeting new people and that I should join. I quickly discovered that Shari has a magnetic personality and immediately makes others feel at ease. Shortly after meeting her, I signed up to take a mixed martial arts fitness class that Shari was teaching out of her home fitness studio, where I laughed and sweated out the stress of being a mother with young children. Years later, we became close when she asked me to help with a fundraiser to support first responders; during that project we bonded over our mutual interests and our passion for striving to do our part in making a difference in our community.

Shari's focus in her personal and professional life is to empower women. Asking me to write the Foreword is an excellent example of this. Even though she knows that I am dyslexic, she trusted that I would write with authenticity and thoughtfulness. Despite my college education and my advanced degree, dyslexia means that I labor over the written word. Professionally, I work as a learning specialist at Hamlin Robinson School — a school specializing in teaching children who have dyslexia and related language difficulties. As a tutor, I ask my students to challenge themselves and I do my best to lead by example. Shari knows from experience that I rarely decline a challenge. As a dyslexic person, I learned at a young age that perseverance through challenges is deeply gratifying. One of the recurring themes found in the *Friendship* series is that growth comes from pushing yourself outside of your comfort zone to take on challenges.

The series consists of interviews of girlfriends who are in Shari's life. One hundred and forty-four different women make up the three-volume series. The conversations between Shari and her girlfriends will remind you of the friends who have come in and out of your own life. Reading and journaling through the first two books of the series, I savored every chapter. These are personal stories of women opening themselves up and being vulnerable by sharing their unique life experiences. Shari also writes her own powerful, thought-provoking, raw reflections, which have led to gratitude for her journey and the growth that she has experienced. At the end of each chapter, there is space to journal.

The first two books contain action steps to incorporate lessons learned into your own life. The three books together are an empowering journey of self-discovery. You will learn about yourself by reflecting on the experiences of others and journaling through the questions at the end of each chapter.

This final book of the *Friendship* series, *Ask Yourself This: Ultimate Life Lessons From And For My Girlfriends*, is designed to challenge you to develop or expand on your own journaling practice. In each chapter, Shari asks her girlfriends simple life questions that evoke conversations that she had never had before, even with some of her life-long girlfriends. As I read these chapters, the conversations deepened thoughts about my own life experiences. Shari's experience with her girlfriends is a testament to how we can learn from our friends through intentional one-on-one conversations. It shows the power that comes from asking questions, listening, practicing active open-mindedness, and finding out what we can learn from our friends. The chapters reflect the uniqueness of each individual and the deep connection we have as women navigating the world. We are reminded of how connected we are as women with relatable and inspiring stories. I'm grateful for the fact that our friendships can provide us with the strength and realizations that can come when we take time to self-reflect through reading and journaling.

Shari is a certified life coach and understands the power of self-reflection. Because I love a challenge, I took her up on the challenge to journal through the entire *Friendship* series. I have found that the process led to affirmations that have helped me lead my best life. I have learned that our life experiences are our greatest teachers, and that resiliency can lead to significant personal growth and happiness. I realize that we are the authors of our own story, and we can choose our mindset to grow and learn from our unique path and to live in gratitude.

— *Kayley Runstad Swan, Learning Specialist, Hamlin Robinson School Learning Center; Board member for Friends of Waterfront Seattle; Board Member and Development Chair for Seattle Academy; member of Seattle University College of Education Advisory Council*

# The Challenge

I.   Commit to the next sixty days. Journaling is the best self-coaching tool available! Over the next sixty days, establish a routine for when you read this book. Choose the same time of day, maybe pour yourself a cup of coffee or tea, and put on your favorite background music. Create your own ritual. This is your time to recharge and work on yourself from the inside out.

2.   As you read through each day, think about the question asked and how your own response is similar to or different from the woman whose story you are reading.

3.   Write more than one-sentence answers. Make your journal notes meaningful. Enjoy this time to really reflect in depth. Write freely without editing; then conclude each journal entry with a significant takeaway, with a provocative thought you want to hold onto. In the process, you'll deepen not only your own understanding of yourself, but also of your friendships.

Bonus: You might want to ask another girlfriend the same questions and learn something new from her life experiences. Or you may even decide to buy this book for a friend and invite her to join you in the challenge, starting on the same day!

#60dayjournalchallenge

# Ask Yourself This

## Childhood

# Day 1

# What did you want to be when you were growing up?

Miriam ("Mim")
Born: Norfolk, Connecticut
Headstone: Be kind and know I love you

Mim and I met about six years ago at a mutual girlfriend's party, and she has since become one of my closest girlfriends. She is a few years younger than I am, with her children in their early teen years while mine are both in their early 20s. I appreciate having girlfriends at different stages of life. The different perspectives and experiences make for rich conversations, as we continue to grow and learn from one another. Mim is someone I can text at any time, and I feel comfortable sharing with her even my most vulnerable self, trusting that she always has my best interest at heart.

*Day 1: What did you want to be when you were growing up?*

Mim and I met outside on a cold January day in Bellevue, Washington. When we met, restaurant regulations due to the covid-19 pandemic allowed seating and service outside, while inside service was prohibited. The restaurant where we chose to meet had a great outdoor space which was tented but with no heaters. By the end of our date, we were both cold — but we ended up having so much fun, especially because we had not gotten out much during the past year due to the pandemic. It felt good to be together despite the chilly air.

Mim's response to the question surprised me. I expected her response to contain a glamorous job title — in part because she is so fashionable and turns heads when she walks into a room. But instead she simply said that as a little girl she dreamed of becoming a mom.

Mim had a childhood that was far from typical. She was born into an Anabaptist community — raised in a compound where all members worked together to provide for the community, including raising their children together. At six weeks of age, children were placed in nurseries — not the large daycare facilities that we have in many of our communities, but nurseries — which held smaller groupings of children. Mim recalls that at just eight years of age, she was a helper in one of the community nurseries. She loved her job as a helper and happily dreamed of becoming a mother when she grew up.

At just seventeen, Mim left the compound to forge her own way in the world. She eventually met and married her husband, becoming a mom at age twenty-seven. Becoming a mother was a dream come true. Mim recalls dressing and wrapping her newborn beautiful baby girl, Gia, in a blanket, laying her down, and simply staring in awe at her. Her little girl was perfection in her eyes. Then two years later she and her husband welcomed their son, Rocco, whom she absolutely adored from the moment she laid eyes on him. Mim's family was now complete. Being a mom felt just as she thought it would: It felt perfect.

In addition to being a mom, Mim has worked in the fitness industry for many years — fitness being her personal passion. Since becoming a mom, she's found work that has allowed her the flexibility to work within her children's schedules. Because her husband has had the same type of work-schedule flexibility, they've worked very well together to ensure that their kids are supported by both parents. While she enjoys working outside of the home, her kids will always be her number-one priority. She realizes how fast they are growing up. At the time we met at the restaurant for this discussion, her children were in the fifth and seventh grade. She is soaking up every minute of these school-aged years.

During the covid-19 pandemic, the studio where she taught fitness classes and worked as a personal trainer closed. Like most parents of school-aged children in our country, she found herself at home helping with remote learning because schools had closed in-person classrooms. Open to new opportunities to use her talents, Mim is looking forward to working outside of the home once again as businesses begin to reopen and the kids return to in-person learning. No matter what her next career move is, being a mom will always be her favorite job in the world — something she dreamed of becoming since she was a child.

Having this conversation with Mim reminded me of the value of being a mother or a mentor to younger people. I love the fact that Mim described being a mom as her childhood dream job. While we push our daughters to become everything a man can be, we must remember to also celebrate her amazing ability to become a mother or a mother figure to a younger person.

# Journal

*Today's date is:*

-----------------------------------------------------------------

*Journal prompt: What did you want to be when you were growing up?*

-----------------------------------------------------------------

-----------------------------------------------------------------

-----------------------------------------------------------------

-----------------------------------------------------------------

-----------------------------------------------------------------

-----------------------------------------------------------------

-----------------------------------------------------------------

-----------------------------------------------------------------

-----------------------------------------------------------------

-----------------------------------------------------------------

-----------------------------------------------------------------

-----------------------------------------------------------------

-----------------------------------------------------------------

-----------------------------------------------------------------

-----------------------------------------------------------------

"Turn those childhood dreams
into the life you dreamed of."
— Shari Leid

Life is like a riding a

bicycle - you must

keep moving forward to

keep your balance.

# Day 2

## Who taught you how to ride a bike?

Julie
Born: Mount Vernon, Washington
Headstone: On to my next journey

Julie and I are first cousins on my mom's side of the family. We are about ten years apart in age and we were raised in different states, which made our times spent together far and few between. But each time we've been together — even as a little girl — I absolutely loved my time with Julie. I am the youngest in our generation of cousins, and as a child, looking up at my older cousins, Julie was the cousin I admired the most. She was the one I wanted to look like and be like. She had a confidence about her that I didn't see in my other family members. While I'm sure she went through her own periods of self-doubt — and she readily admits that she had some stumbles along the way — she has always done things on her own terms, which to this day I continue to fiercely admire.

*Day 2: Who taught you how to ride a bike?*

This question pulled at Julie's heart strings. She was immediately taken back to when she was just four years old. She remembers the day clearly. In her mind's eye she pictures her dad's face — his laughter and patience — while he taught her how to ride a bicycle. She remembers the sheer joy on his face when he witnessed her pedaling on her own. While it is said that you never forget how to ride a bike, I'm pretty sure it can also be said that you'll never forget who taught you how to ride a bike. And I'd bet that ninety-nine percent of the time, that person was someone very instrumental in your life — and that learning to ride a bike was just one of many life lessons that that significant person taught you.

Julie's dad, my uncle, passed away just over a decade ago. He stood out to me amongst my mom's eight older brothers. He was the fifth from the oldest of the brothers, and one of the easier, more social brothers to talk to. It is not hard for me to picture him as the patient father who was easy to talk to and always had a ready smile — just as Julie describes. Julie misses him. He was the person in her family whom she was the closest to. As we were talking, I could see a lot of similar personality traits and a physical resemblance between Julie and her dad. It was a reminder that he lives on through her.

Learning to ride a bike symbolizes a child's first experience of freedom and independence. It symbolizes overcoming a challenge and taking a leap of faith. I can picture the day Julie describes, as it takes me back to my own memory of the day I learned to ride a bike. That day for me was not too different from the day that Julie remembers with her own dad. I also picture a warm sunny day. I can feel the gentle patience, instruction, and joy that my own dad shared with me as he taught me how to ride. While I imagine that our dads recognized the day their little girls learned to ride a bike as one of life's big milestones, I wonder what it was like for them to experience a tiny sense of letting go just a bit, giving their daughters a gentle push towards independence.

Being taught to ride a bike by a parent — in our case, our dads — is one of the greatest gifts our fathers ever gave us. They not only taught us a skill that could be quite scary at first, but they also taught us how to pick ourselves up when we fall, to trust ourselves to be able to overcome a challenge, and to have faith in our abilities.

Who taught you how to ride a bike? Was it a sibling, a parent, a neighbor, an uncle, an aunt, a grandparent, or a cousin? I bet it was someone important — someone you will never forget.

# Journal

*Today's date is:*

_____

*Journal prompt: Who taught you how to ride a bike?*

_____

_____

_____

_____

_____

_____

_____

_____

_____

_____

_____

_____

_____

_____

_____

_____

"At age six, my dad taught me how
to ride a bike and that is when I
became an invincible superhero."
— Shari Leid

# *Day 3*

# Describe your parents. What do you love about them?

Angela
Born: New York City
Headstone: She was a spark for others

I was so excited to meet up with Angela, because up until this time, we had never met in person. Even though we had not met before, my relationship with her dates to over a decade ago when I stumbled across Savor Seattle (www.SavorSeattleTours.com), a tour company in Seattle that Angela owned and operated. My children were grade-school-aged at the time, and I booked a couple of the tours for family fun days, along with a pub tour for just my husband and me. When friends and family members came to town, I always suggested a Savor Seattle food tour of Seattle's iconic Pike Place Market. Savor Seattle was consistently rated number one on many of the popular tour and review sites — not a surprise given how great the tour guides she hired were. It was a go-to for locals and visitors alike — with structured tours that included fabulous city insights, fun, and food.

*Day 3: Describe your parents. What do you love about them?*

Angela's parents immigrated from China. Her mom and dad are from the same city, Fuzhou, a place known for entrepreneurship. Angela explained to me that it is common in the United States to find that when you are at a Chinese restaurant or at a Chinese-owned business, the business owners are from Fuzhou and speak Foochow, a dialect of that city.

Angela immediately described her parents as being opposites. At the time of our meeting, her parents had been married for about forty-two years. She wonders how they managed in the early years of their marriage given how opposite their personalities are. However, Angela can now see how over the years their opposite nature has worked in their favor. Her mom's risk-averse nature balances out her father's entrepreneurial adventurous spirit.

Angela refers to her parents as her North Star. She believes she received the best from both: her dad's spirit of adventure balanced by her mom's cautious nature. She sees that this has contributed to much of her success as an entrepreneur. Angela's background is in marketing and branding. A graduate of the Wharton School of Business at the University of Pennsylvania, she always planned to run her own business. When she moved to Seattle, she began her tour company. As mentioned earlier, her company was a success, consistently ranked the number-one food tour company in Seattle year after year.

When the covid-19 pandemic hit, Angela's tour business was literally shut down overnight. She immediately moved into troubleshooting mode and ideas in her head began to churn. She called her parents in tears about the sudden shut-down, emotions stemming not only from concern for what she needed to do to save her business, but also concern for the employees she had to lay off and the many food vendors her company supported. She shared with her parents an idea: Why not bring some of the iconic Pike Place Market vendors to homes — in the form of a curated weekly food box?

It was a huge undertaking and one that would require hours of logistics to manage. The logistics ranged from finding box and container suppliers, to locating a space to assemble the boxes, to working with small food vendors and restaurants — which were not really set up for a mass-delivery service. Not to mention the fact that she needed to find the customers.

Her father's response was, "What is the worst that can happen?" He emphasized that she had her health and her family — which were the most important things. He reminded her that money can always be made.

Angela decided to go for it. To anyone on the sidelines watching, she made the switch from an in-person tour business to a specialty food delivery service appear seamless. I myself immediately signed up to receive the weekly boxes — and they quickly became the highlight of my week during our city's stay-at-home mandate. For many weeks, the only time I ventured out of my home was for the curbside pick-up of my Savor Seattle Pike Place Market food box. It was Springtime when the boxes first became available, so they included flowers from Pike Place Market's flower vendors. I was able to order extra blossoms each week and then I dropped off bouquets at friends' home porches as a pandemic pick-me-up on my drive back home from Pike Place Market.

Angela's business grew and the demand became greater each week. She eventually began a local delivery service and even designed curated boxes that were available to ship nationwide. Not only were each week's boxes specially chosen with different weekly items, but she also provided specialty boxes — supporting women-owned businesses, Black American chefs, LGBTQ communities, American democracy (with fun election-themed boxes), and much more.

While Angela made the transition look easy from the outside, it was not easy in the least. At one point she was working eighty hours a week — doing everything from curating to marketing and branding to assembly. She was able to hire back half of her tour staff, which meant that the people she hired back were now doing jobs that didn't truly match their background and training; yet the excitement of the growing business gave them energy to carry the new business model to the next level.

The new model not only kept Angela in business, but it also kept many of the small restaurants and food vendors in the Pike Place Market afloat. This was all happening while many other businesses, especially restaurants in Seattle, were shutting down left and right. It is hard to grasp the total effect Angela's curated boxes have had on the local economy as many new customers were able to discover restaurants and vendors through the weekly boxes that they might never have heard of otherwise. I imagine many customers like me will now venture out post-pandemic to these new beloved Pike Place Market finds to experience them in person.

Angela's work has not gone unnoticed, as she was featured by several business outlets and in the mainstream media. To top it all off, just ten months after her pivotal bold switch, she was made an offer that she could not refuse: Her company was purchased by a larger company that intends to continue the work she began.

Following the sale of her business, Angela has not sat idle. In addition to her continued work with Savor Seattle during its ownership transition, she has taken on the position of Chief Brand Officer for Team Building, a national company that provides virtual, in-person, and hybrid team-building experiences. Angela also started a new business in 2022 in response to the #VeryAsian movement, Domo Collective Jewelry. Domo Collective is a marketplace for foodie jewelry by Asian makers with a percent of each sale donated to the Very Asian Foundation.

As Angela reflects on the personality traits she inherited from each of her parents — the risk-taker and the risk-avoider — she is thankful for the balance they've provided her. She credits them for much of who she is today. Listening to Angela's story makes me wonder what my children feel they have received from my husband and me. I realize the importance of how much we as parents lead by example.

Ever since Angela told me her dad's motto in life, I've found that I've adopted this as my own. I hear the words repeatedly in my head: "What is the worst that can happen?"

# Journal

*Today's date is:*

_____

*Journal prompt: Describe your parents. What do you love about them?*

_____

_____

_____

_____

_____

_____

_____

_____

_____

_____

_____

_____

_____

_____

_____

"Speak to your children in the way
you want to be remembered."
— Shari Leid

I wish my dad had lived long enough to have met my children – I know being a grandparent would have been his favorite role in life.

# Day 4

## What is your happiest memory from childhood?

Michelle
Born: San Rafael, California
Headstone: Lying here is a heart of gold

Michelle and I met at the same party where I met Mim (Day 1). Although we initially met about six years ago, it has been during the past couple of years that we have had the opportunity to get to know one another, getting together outside of larger gatherings. Michelle is a talented interior designer with a flair for beauty and style. She has a tight-knit group of girlfriends who have been with her through thick and thin, each one knowing that they can count on the other for love and support whenever called upon. When I think of Michelle, I not only think of her devotion to her friends but also of her fierce love for her children — which she has captured beautifully in photographs throughout the years.

*Day 4: What is your happiest memory from childhood?*

When Michelle and I met for this conversation, indoor dining had just opened in the Seattle area at twenty-five-percent capacity following many weeks of an indoor-dining ban due to the covid-19 pandemic. Because of the more relaxed regulations, we were able to sit inside the restaurant, which was welcome, given it had been pouring rain all day long. We were the only ones on our side of the place, with no one within twenty feet of us. This fact made the dining experience feel very safe. It was my first-time dining inside a restaurant in months — a sliver of normalcy following a difficult year of social distancing.

I love that Michelle's face naturally lit up when she began to share her favorite childhood memory. It was incredibly special to hear her talk about her grandmother, her mom's mom. Michelle called her Nana. She remembers that as a little girl, she would often go to Nana's home, which was about an hour's drive from her childhood home. Michelle lived with her parents in the Bay Area of California and her Nana resided in Palo Alto. Michelle described the days she spent with Nana with such warmth and detail, I swear I could picture it as if I were watching her wonderful childhood memories unfold right in front of me.

Her Nana's home had an outdoor pool. Michelle remembers how she would spend all day swimming and playing. She recalls the yummy grape sodas that her Nana would bring out to her. She remembers being carefree and having Nana all to herself. As Michelle described the scene of these warm days in her Nana's pool, I pictured a little girl filled with joy and confidence, without any worry or self-doubt.

Michelle remembers going into town with Nana and feeling special. Nana would allow her to pick out a new dress at a children's boutique — which no longer exists but at the time it was the fanciest store in town. Adding to these fun days were trips to A&W Root Beer, where the servers wore roller skates and came out to the cars to take orders and deliver food. Looking back at this memory, Michelle realizes that it must not have been the restaurant of choice for Nana, but she went there simply because she knew how much fun that atmosphere was for a child.

Michelle shared with me the difference between her relationship with Nana and her relationship with her grandparents on the other side of her family. While she loved them unconditionally and knows that they loved her and they were always very kind, when she visited them, they simply did not engage with her the way Nana did.

Hearing Michelle's recollection of her special time with Nana helped me realize how important it is to give the gift of time to the children in our lives, to make sure that they feel special and loved. Michelle's story is a testament to how much power we have as adults to shape the lives of the children we have in our care. To give the gift of happy memories that will last a lifetime to a child, we simply need to put away our own distractions for a few hours and focus on them.

# Journal

*Today's date is:*

-------------------------------------------------------------------

*Journal prompt: What is your happiest memory from childhood?*

-------------------------------------------------------------------

-------------------------------------------------------------------

-------------------------------------------------------------------

-------------------------------------------------------------------

-------------------------------------------------------------------

-------------------------------------------------------------------

-------------------------------------------------------------------

-------------------------------------------------------------------

-------------------------------------------------------------------

-------------------------------------------------------------------

-------------------------------------------------------------------

-------------------------------------------------------------------

-------------------------------------------------------------------

-------------------------------------------------------------------

"Nothing beats the joy of a happy childhood memory."

— Shari Leid

# Day 5

## What's one family tradition you'd like to carry on in the future?

Sabrina
Born: Chicago
Headstone: Na, na, na, na, na, na — Hey, hey, goodbye

Sabrina and I met about four years ago when we were both recent transplants to Woodinville, Washington. Sabrina, her husband, and young son moved from California to Woodinville with the intent to open a winery. Woodinville is one of three areas of Washington state that is known for its stellar tasting rooms and wineries. They are now proud owners of Prohibition Cellars (www.prohibitioncellars.com), a winery that has rapidly developed a reputation among wine connoisseurs for remarkable wines.

*Day 5: What's one family tradition you'd like to carry on in the future?*

I must admit that because Sabrina's husband was born and raised in Hungary and Sabrina's parents immigrated from Hungary, I assumed she would be knee-deep in Hungarian family traditions. However, she surprised me when she shared that her first thought when the question was posed was that she has *no* family traditions that she practices, let alone any that she hoped her son would carry on.

Nevertheless, while thinking further about it, she began to realize that she does indeed have a family tradition — a very important one. Her family tradition involves connecting and deepening the rich bonds with both her and her husband's extended family and with Hungary, her husband's homeland. This is one tradition that they are passing down to their young son.

Having grown up in Hungary, Sabrina's husband has fond memories of spending entire Summers at his family's lake house, on the same street where many of his life-long childhood friends also resided — playing outside, eating together, laughing, and sharing stories. One of the most important traditions that happened both at his home and at the lake house — which carries on to this day in Hungary — is the Sunday family meal. As Sabrina described this tradition to me, I felt like I was transported to Hungary and seated right at that family table with her and her husband's family.

"Having Sunday family lunches together is one of our favorite and most important family traditions," Sabrina told me. "Sandor grew up with Sunday family lunches being part of his tradition, which carried over from home to the lake house. Cooking always begins first thing Sunday morning, and the entire family sits down at the table exactly at noon when lunch is ready. Everything else that day is organized around the lunch. Always, we start with soup, followed by a main course with multiple sides and salads, crowned by dessert and a shot of espresso. Sandor's grandma used to make these meals. Now it's Sandor's dad and mom. And one day it will be Sandor — or one of his sisters — to do the cooking. And this Summer — God willing — there will literally be a span of 100 years and three generations at the table! Sandor's grandma is 100 years old, and her youngest great-grandchild is just a few months old.

"It is maintaining these big family gatherings that is most important to our family," Sabrina now realizes. "These Sunday lunches at the lake house are usually no less than fifteen people, but it can be twenty-one if all the siblings and their families attend. In fact, when Sandor's parents renovated the lake house, the design was literally centered around the most important areas of our growing family: the kitchen and patio where we all eat and congregate."

Sabrina, although born and raised in the United States, also has similar memories of her own gatherings with family in Hungary. As mentioned earlier, both her parents immigrated to the United States. They arrived in America in 1956, met a few years later, and married in 1967. At the time Sabrina was born, Hungary was under Communist rule, which made it unavailable for easy visits. However, by the time Sabrina was nine years old, Communist rule had fallen, so she was able to make her first trip to Hungary with her family. This first visit was the beginning of visits every other Summer. By age eleven, she began taking the flight from the United States to Hungary on her own. She loved the Summers that she spent in Hungary, being surrounded by aunts, uncles, and cousins. With these visits, she fell in love with the country of her ancestors. By the time she was in high school, Sabrina knew she wanted to attend college in Hungary, which she did, and it was during that time that she met Sandor.

Now, as a mother, she, along with her husband, has started the tradition of Summer visits to Hungary for their young son,

Oliver. Her son is growing up understanding his roots and knowing his relatives. He is experiencing the land, the food, and the culture of Hungary. These experiences are providing him with a strong sense of identity, pride, and belonging.

Sabrina's story reminds me that traditions give us something more than just a blueprint to follow or something to do simply out of habit; they can provide us with an important understanding of who we are and our unique and worthy place in the world.

# Journal

*Today's date is:*

_____

*Journal prompt: What's one family tradition you'd like to carry on in the future?*

_____

_____

_____

_____

_____

_____

_____

_____

_____

_____

_____

_____

_____

_____

_____

# *Day 6*

## What are you most scared of losing, and what would you truly lose if you lost it?

Arlene
Born: Cavite, Philippines (on a U.S. Navy base)
Headstone: Be. Live life. Unconditionally love.

Arlene and I attended the same high school for a short period of time but did not know one another in school. I attended the school for just seven months and knew who Arlene was. She was popular, a cheerleader, and one of the prettiest girls in the class. It was impossible not to know Arlene. Having many of the same high-school friends, we later connected on Facebook, and over the years we just naturally got to know each other through social media, eventually hanging out in person. As is often the case, because we grew up knowing many of the same people, we naturally found an easy rhythm to our friendship. Meeting with Arlene now feels like meeting with a childhood friend, even though our friendship was really formed only a few years ago.

*Day 6: What are you most scared of losing, and what would you truly lose if you lost it?*

Arlene and I met up at Victory Lounge (www.instagram.com/victoryloungesea), a well-known Seattle bar that she and her husband own. Because we met before the bar opened for the evening, it was empty, and we had a chance to catch up without any distractions. We had not seen each other since my fiftieth birthday party, over a year prior. My birthday party had so many people in attendance that it was a real gift to have this one-on-one time with Arlene.

When we sat down, I asked Arlene how her family was managing through the covid-19 pandemic. In addition to Victory Lounge, they are part owners of a music venue, El Corazón (www.elcorazonseattle.com), as well as another eating establishment, Big Bubba's Burgers (www.bigbubbasburgers.net). Their music venue remained closed throughout the pandemic, and Victory Lounge adapted according to the regulations that were constantly in flux during the past year. As I watched many restaurants and venues in the Seattle area and nationwide permanently close due to the economic hardships the pandemic had wrought, I was concerned for friends like Arlene who were in the struggling hospitality business. While I expected her to answer my questions by talking about the challenges of the businesses, her immediate response instead was to talk about the blessings that her family has — including their home and health.

She said that the first thing that came to her mind was the health of her family — her husband and two sons. When I pressed on the latter part of the question — asking what she would truly lose if she lost her family — she had a hard time putting it into words. Finally, her answer was simply, "Me." Arlene went on to explain that nothing matters more than the health of the people she loves.

I joked that while I expected her to immediately mention her kids in her answer, I didn't expect her to mention her husband first. Arlene proceeded to share the story of their relationship. It was refreshing to see how in love she is with her husband — even after years of marriage, working together, and raising two children. It made me think that while we may advise our daughters and girlfriends to make sure they are always independent despite their partner, we should also celebrate the value of finding a life partner you can't imagine living without.

One of the things I love about these conversations is that you never know where the teaching points will lead. This talk with Arlene taught me that it is not a weakness to find someone you couldn't imagine living your life without. In fact, that should be the goal when finding a life partner. While it is important to have a sense of self and to have the ability to survive on your own, there is also an incredible beauty in loving someone to the point where it is hard for you to imagine your life any other way. Having this mindset keeps gratitude and grace in the relationship, especially when it comes to our long-term relationships — which can easily become stagnant and lost if not properly nourished. We should never take our relationships with the people we love for granted.

# Journal

*Today's date is:*

---

*Journal prompt: What are you most scared of losing, and what would you truly lose if you lost it?*

---

"I know my family so well; I can tell who is coming into a room just by the sound of their footsteps."
— Shari Leid

*Day 7*

# What are the three most important things that children should be taught in school?

Melissa
Born: West Covina, California
Headstone: Loving mother and companion,
Joyful warrior,
Seeker of what is good each day.
You are powerful beyond measure.

I met Melissa over a decade ago when I ran a personal fitness studio out of the basement of my home. Melissa's eldest child, her son, was a toddler at the time and she was working for a large non-profit organization. When I'd introduce Melissa to my other clients, I often described her as the busiest person I know. I was always inspired that despite her full schedule, she carved out those precious evening hours to join me at my studio five days a week. The workouts were a mix of strength training and mixed martial arts drills, which allowed Melissa to punch and kick, and physically and mentally release the days' stressors. During our meeting for this book, she shared with me the power and strength that those workouts gave her.

*Day 7: What are the three most important things that children should be taught in school?*

As Melissa and I had not connected outside of social media in such a long time — probably close to ten years — I had forgotten that she received her doctorate from Harvard Graduate School of Education. She was the perfect person to ask about what children should be learning in school.

Melissa's answer surprised me. She began with, "Children need to learn how to learn."

She explained that while children can become good at test-taking or finishing their homework assignments, they often leave school lacking the skill set to become life-long learners. Children don't just need to know where to find the answers; they also need to learn how to ask questions, to go deeper, and to take chances. When children begin to ask questions, they begin to see outside of their immediate world, and they can think on a global scale. They not only learn that something is important, but they gain an understanding of why it is important.

When they learn how to learn, they become empowered; they are not afraid to move forward and try something new. Through this process, children will find that being wrong is sometimes as important to learning as being right. Lifetime learners will never become bored with life. Maintaining their curiosity, they will have a much easier time finding their place in the world.

The second-most important thing that Melissa believes

children should be taught in school is communication. According to Melissa, communication is key to success in life. In today's technology-focused world, students have their heads buried in their electronic devices and communicate without moving away from them. Often schoolwork — including communication with peers and teachers — is now being conducted via electronic tablets and computers rather than face to face. The art of looking someone in the eye and carrying on a conversation in an effective manner is being lost. When school budgets are cut, often programs such as physical education, the arts, and recess time become casualties. These casualties are profound because these activities provide the greatest opportunities for learning the art and skill of face-to-face communication.

Finally, the third thing that Melissa would like to add to the school curriculum is learning how to work together. I mentioned to her that I grew up during the busing era of Seattle schools — where the children in the wealthier neighborhoods, typically White kids, were bused to the poorer neighborhoods, and the children in the poorer neighborhoods, typically kids of color, were bused to the more affluent neighborhoods. That busing experience has led to an entire Seattle generation of middle-aged and older adults who are comfortable working alongside a person of a different background because they had that experience as children.

While Melissa wasn't necessarily suggesting busing as the means to teach the art of working together, the skill of being able to work with any group of people to find solutions is something vital in our society. It would not only benefit the workplace, but also the family, the neighborhood, and the whole community. In fact, the benefits would be felt globally.

Introducing Melissa's ideas in schools is a dream that could and should come true, but it will take the reworking of many institutional systems. While these changes may not take place in our lifetime, as parents and mentors we have the power right now to begin — by establishing these ideas ourselves, in our homes. The benefits for the next generation are immeasurable.

# Journal

Today's date is:

_____

Journal prompt: What are the three most important things that children should be taught in school?

_____

_____

_____

_____

_____

_____

_____

_____

_____

_____

_____

_____

_____

_____

_____

_____

_____

# *Ask Yourself This*

# Childhood:
# Shari's Own Reflections

I. *What did you want to be when you were growing up?* A teacher. I was blessed with an amazing first experience in school. I loved my kindergarten teacher, Ms. Dumas, who taught at Brighton Elementary School in Seattle. My first-grade teacher, Ms. Ghan, also at Brighton Elementary, was excellent. She celebrated my math and reading skills. She made me feel special by lending me books that I could take home, books that were above my grade level. These books came from her own collection, which she kept in her teacher's closet; this made me feel like the smartest kid on the planet. At the time, I couldn't imagine growing up to be anything other than the two women I admired most.

It wasn't until I became the mother of a child who struggled in school with significant learning challenges that I realized how fortunate I was — not only to be blessed without those challenges but also to have had teachers who instilled the love of learning and school at such a young age.

Unfortunately, it wasn't until college that my daughter had my childhood experience. She called me one evening, during her sophomore year of college, to share that when she advised one of her professors of her education accommodations, the professor responded by saying that she was very happy to have my daughter in her class. My daughter was elated. I'm glad that she was finally able to experience the power of how much a teacher's appreciation can inspire learning and confidence.

I'm now living my childhood dream. As a life coach for women, I am a teacher — just in a different form from what I imagined as a child.

2. *Who taught you how to ride a bike?* My dad. Like Julie (Day 2), thinking about this day brings a smile to my face as I picture how happy my father was when I was able to conquer this skill. I don't recall my exact age, but I was probably in kindergarten or first grade. My first bike was a hand-me-down from my mom's friend's older daughter. It was red with hard solid tires, rather than traditional bike tires that require air. It was quite unattractive, so I was very happy to receive another hand-me-down bicycle a couple of years later: a purple Schwinn banana-seat bicycle. The seat had glitter sparkles and the handlebars were adorned with tassels, and I thought it was the most beautiful bicycle in the world. I was fearless on that bike, often riding on the handlebars as my friends pedaled quickly down streets — crashing on more than one occasion. When I think back to it, riding my bicycle around the neighborhood was my first experience with self-reliance and freedom — a very happy part of my childhood.

3. *Describe your parents. What do you love about them?* I talk a lot about my relationship with my dad and much less about my relationship with my mom. I decided to switch things up and dedicate this answer to her. I have a lot to appreciate about her, which I've neglected to share in prior writings. I have focused on the struggles that exist in our relationship. But when I think back to my childhood, she always had homemade meals ready for my dad and me; she was also my reliable taxi to and from school and all the extracurricular activities, often waiting patiently in the car or sitting on the sidelines at my sports practices or piano lessons. She is a strong person. As of this writing, she is ninety-three years old. She lived through the internment of her family during World War II; she survived isolation at a retirement home during the covid-19 pandemic. She drove until she was ninety years of age, and she has been in overall good health most of her life.

   I joke that she and I vote at every election simply to cancel out each other's votes. It is rare that we see eye to eye, which used to fill me with so much anger and resentment towards her that I was blinded to her strengths. I'm fortunate that we have both lived long enough that I can appreciate and admire the strong person that she is, despite our differences. I am glad that we were able to create a relationship of mutual respect before it was too late.

4. *What is your happiest memory from childhood?* I was once asked this in a podcast interview. Prior to that, I had never looked back to define such a moment. Like Michelle (Day 4), my happiest memory is focused on a relationship. The happiest memory

I have from childhood is the times I made my dad laugh. He was so intelligent, with the sharpest wit. I loved how his face lit up when I made him laugh. My dad's spontaneous laughter is really my happiest childhood memory.

My children never met my dad. He died of a massive heart attack in January 2001, coincidentally on my mom's birthday. My husband and I brought our adopted daughter home from China just six months later in June of 2001, and our son was born in March of 2002. My heart hurts when I think about how much my kids would have loved my dad, and how he would have loved the experience of being a grandfather.

5. *What's one family tradition you'd like to carry on in the future?* I was not raised with family traditions. My parents who adopted me were born in Washington state, and they were wrongfully relocated and detained during WWII when Japanese legal immigrants and Japanese Americans who resided on the West Coast were placed into internment camps simply because of their Japanese blood. As such, my father purposely raised me without a tie to family traditions, since his experience with being of Japanese descent was a negative one. My mother was the second-youngest of ten children and was also not raised with family traditions that likely would have existed for her parents when they grew up in Japan. As such, they passed none on to me and I had no family traditions to pass to my children.

However, one tradition that my husband and I have had the fortune of *creating* for our children was that we would take an annual Summer trip to a country that we as a family had never visited. By the time our kids were out of high school, they had experienced travel to Mexico, Canada, Peru, Panama, China, Hong Kong, Vietnam, Laos, Cambodia, Italy, Scotland, South Africa, South Korea, and Australia. I would love it if when they became parents, they carry on this tradition for their kids. It wouldn't have to be a new country — but at least a new city or state. There is so much learning that comes from travel, which is very special and unique.

6. *What are you most scared of losing, and what would you truly lose if you lost it?* The easy answer is, "My kids." The loss is so unimaginable that I do not have words to describe what I would truly lose. Outside of that easy answer, I am most scared of losing my mind to disease or injury. It is not a fear that I think of very often, but it is what pops up for me. This is a motivating factor that reminds me to appreciate each day and to use the gift of my mind's ability to the fullest.

7. *What are the three most important things that children should be taught in school?* How to thoughtfully ask questions, letter-writing (not texting) skills, and conflict management. I believe that the teaching of effective communication and relationship skills has been sadly lacking in our schools.

# Ask Yourself This

## High School and College Years

# *Day 8*

# Where in your life do you feel misunderstood?

Mayumi
Born: Georgia, United States
Headstone: [DOB] resilience [DOD]

Mayumi and I have over 500 mutual friends on Facebook. Of those mutual friends, we probably personally know more than half of them; and out of those friends, it probably boils down to just a handful we would refer to as our very close girlfriends — the women we can reach out to at any time. We have a couple of other similarities. Perhaps the most powerful is that we each have a complicated relationship with our mom. Mayumi is Blasian, i.e., she is the daughter of an Asian mom who is from Japan and a Black dad from America. Mayumi's dad died when she was just two, and she was taken to Japan and raised there until she and her mom returned to the States, where Mayumi entered the first grade, speaking only Japanese.

While I'm not Blasian (or Whasian — a White Asian), I was raised by Japanese American parents who adopted me — a full Korean orphan — from Korea. Both Mayumi and I grew up raised by Japanese mothers, feeling that we were never fully accepted by them. Mayumi was never Japanese enough or Black enough; and I was never Japanese enough or Korean enough. We grew up at a time where mixed races and international and interracial adoptions were not celebrated as they commonly are today.

*Day 8: Where in your life do you feel misunderstood?*

Mayumi's quick one-word answer to the question I posed was, "Everywhere." Mayumi grew up being misunderstood because of her appearance. Still to this day, people assume she is this or that, ranging from positive to negative — simply because of her appearance. Mayumi is an attractive woman — a former model, a Mrs. Washington pageant winner, a lifestyle mentor, an author, a motivational speaker, and an entrepreneur. She always has a new project brewing (www.mayumimuller.com). When Mayumi was a child and even into her teen years, the mainstream media did not have models and celebrities who looked like Mayumi. In many of the places she lived, she looked different from the other kids because of her biracial background. She didn't fit into the Black community or the Japanese community, simply because of the way she looked.

It's hard to imagine Mayumi ever looking awkward. Her husband will testify — based on the photos he has seen of her in her teenage years — that she didn't go through an awkward period. However, Mayumi did share a story with me: that her mom paid a friend's son to take her to a couple of important high school dances. She has come into her own and aged incredibly well. She is the author of *Mayumi's Secret: Fcking Fab & Fit After 40*. People often assume things come easy for her — again based on her appearance. They don't realize all the hard work she puts in each day, which is the foundation of her success.

Much of her drive has come from being misjudged. She has taken judgment and turned it into a motivator to succeed. Her passion for her own success has also led her to champion women to rise above judgment and to come into their power. She is quick to point out that she didn't get to this place in life, being completely comfortable in her own skin, entirely on her own. Her husband is her best friend. She credits him with a lot of her growth in the past ten years. In partnership with him, she has been able to see herself through his eyes — beautiful just as she is.

I asked Mayumi if she thought that as women, we could do this for our girlfriends — help them see themselves as we see them — beautiful just as they are.

She responded, "Absolutely. We can support our girlfriends and support their growth."

Mayumi shared that while experiencing a lot of personal and professional growth in the last ten years, she lost friends — friends who didn't want to accept her when her priorities shifted and her mindset changed. While losing friends was initially difficult, she quickly realized that she needed to surround herself with individuals who not only allow her to grow but who also celebrate that growth with her.

We can never allow being misunderstood to define us.

# Journal

*Today's date is:*

---

*Journal prompt: Where in your life do you feel misunderstood?*

---

---

---

---

---

---

---

---

---

---

---

---

---

---

---

"Who are all these old people?
Oh, they are people I was in high
school with!"
— Shari Leid

# *Day 9*

# What career advice would you give your sixteen-year-old self?

Kim
Born: Seattle
Headstone: Would the last person please turn off the lights?

I met Kim through her childhood best friend, CC. To be honest, when I first met Kim, I wasn't sure if she liked me. I remember attempting to start a conversation with her, but her responses were short, which led me to believe that she wasn't interested in getting to know me. However, just like many first impressions, my assumption was wrong. Thankfully, I didn't allow my misinterpretation of our first meeting stop me from inviting her to a holiday cookie exchange party at my home, because I was pleasantly surprised when she responded that she was attending, even when she didn't know a single soul. The theme of the party was *Where's Waldo?* She put on her best *Where's Waldo* look and walked into a group of about eighty women. It really was one of the most courageous acts I've ever witnessed because I knew in that moment that Kim was pushing herself outside of her comfort zone.

*Day 9: What career advice would you give your sixteen-year-old self?*

Kim grew up in the Central District ("The CD") of Seattle, an area that was once the hub for Black families, Black businesses, and Black culture. In fact, for decades it was one of the only areas in Seattle where you would find a Black business — in part due to the neighborhood racial covenants that existed in Seattle prior to the Civil Rights Movement. Kim grew up in this area of Seattle where everyone seemed to know each other, knew one another's families, and knew each other's business. Just like many of the residents in The CD, she barely ventured out of her area of Seattle as a child — and didn't realize until she was a teen and young adult, the negative light that was cast upon The CD and its residents by the rest of Seattle.

The stigma of how she was seen based solely on her race and on the area of the city she grew up in — this burden subconsciously affected her self-esteem and her ability to see herself in a career of authority. Now, in her 40s, she looks back at her life and realizes that in the past she took jobs just for the paycheck and did not seek additional opportunities — nor did she leave jobs when she should have. She viewed herself as a worker, confined to the duties outlined in the job description. She limited her experience and opportunities, falling into the trap of allowing others' misperceptions to define her.

So, if Kim could go back and sit down with her sixteen-year-old self, she would tell that young teen that it is imperative that she look for opportunities in every job — that she look beyond the basic duties required of the job. She would counsel her sixteen-year-old self not to be defined by the limitations that others want to put on her, especially when she finds herself as the only Black person in the room.

Speaking with Kim made me realize how important it is as parents that we have these conversations with our children — to remind them not to allow themselves to be limited by anyone else's beliefs. I love that while Kim can't go back to her sixteen-year-old self, in her 40s she is rewriting the messages she received as a youth and young adult. She is making sure that she now sees opportunities rather than limitations. When those old self-defeating messages appear, she can pause and challenge herself to take a step outside of her comfort zone.

Listening to Kim's story has prompted me to look in the mirror and ask myself, "What story have I let others write for me? And how can I rewrite that story and make it my own?"

# Journal

*Today's date is:*

---

*Journal prompt: What career advice would you give your sixteen-year-old self?*

---

---

---

---

---

---

---

---

---

---

---

---

---

"Do what you love, and you'll feel the joy of aligning with your true self."
— Shari Leid

# Day 10

## If you could time-travel back to an earlier time in your life, where would you visit and what would you do?

Tracey
Born: Seattle
Headstone: Joining angels gone before,
shining light on angels left behind

Tracey and I met through social media. We noticed on Facebook that we share many mutual friends, not just virtual friends but real flesh-and-blood friends. Recognizing all our connections, Tracey reached out to introduce herself. It seemed inevitable that we'd meet in person. Now, we see one another often, including at the celebrations and events hosted by those mutual friends that I mentioned, and I consider her to be one of my dearest friends. She has a fabulous way of taking time for friends and family while being very active as managing director of a Bellevue, Washington weight-loss and healthy lifestyle facility (www.evolve180weightloss.com).

*Day 10: If you could time-travel back to an earlier time in your life, where would you visit and what would you do?*

If Tracey could time travel, she would go back to her senior year in high school. At seventeen years old, the world around her as she knew it was crumbling. It was during her senior year that her mom, who was only thirty-nine years of age, and a mother of four — with Tracey being the second oldest — was diagnosed with brain cancer. The time between the diagnosis and her untimely death was not very long — only months. A high school year usually defined by celebration and excitement was now forever defined by heartache, confusion, and grief.

When Tracey thinks back to who she was at seventeen, it feels to her as if she is looking back at an entirely different person. She barely recognizes herself. She recalls feeling a sense of overconfidence. She believed that now that her mom had died, she was free to do anything she wanted to do since she had no one to tell her *no*. Her parents had divorced when she was ten years old, and her dad — who was also relatively young — was absorbed in his own life and not there for her and her three siblings the way she needed him to be. The members of her extended family on her mother's side were also grieving terribly, and due to their own profound grief, they were not able to show up in the way the kids needed them. Tracey began making life choices that a seventeen-year-old without guidance might do. She focused only on what she desired to do at the time rather than on what actions she could do to prepare for the future.

Tracey started to rebel against what may have been expected of her had her mom not gotten sick and died. She decided to forgo college and instead chose to live in the moment — which included moving to Oahu from Seattle. She waitressed and enjoyed her independence before finally returning home. When she got back home to Washington state, she began a relationship and became pregnant with her first child. Although she was young and unwed, she welcomed the pregnancy, always knowing that she wanted to be a mom. In fact, being a mother was much more of a priority in life for Tracey than getting married. Thinking back, she wonders if experiencing her parents' divorce and seeing her parents involved in different relationships influenced her disinterest in marriage at the time.

While Tracey isn't one to live with regrets, when she reflects upon this tender time in her life, she wonders what her life would have been like if her mom hadn't died — or if the adults around her had been more present to guide her. She suspects she may have gone to college, and her life journey might have taken a much different path. So, if she could go back in time, she would go back to the age of seventeen and try to connect with the adults around her to seek their guidance.

I asked Tracey, given her experience, what advice she would give to adults who lose friends with teenage or young adult children.

She advised, "Stay in that child's life — even if that child is out of high school. A young person, in their late teens and early 20s, still needs that parental guidance, even when they think they can make it on their own."

Speaking with Tracey reminds me of a conversation I had with a friend in my second book, *Make Your Mess Your Message: More Life Lessons From And For My Girlfriends* — with a woman who lost her mom in high school and her father in her early 20s. One piece of advice she gave to those who lose parents was to stay close to your parents' friends because they were a part of your parents' lives. Her advice — coupled with Tracey's wish to stay connected to her mom's friends — reminds me of the important role a community can play in a child's and young adult's life. The teenagers and young adults who are in our lives aren't as independent as we may think. They can use the guidance of older adults around them, even when they don't realize it.

# Journal

*Today's date is:*

_____

*Journal prompt: If you could time-travel back to an earlier time in your life, where would you visit and what would you do?*

_____

_____

_____

_____

_____

_____

_____

_____

_____

_____

_____

_____

_____

_____

_____

_____

# Day 11

## What choice has had the greatest impact on your life?

Karen
Born: Seattle
Headstone: She always tried to be kind

K aren and I met shortly after we moved to the same area of Washington state, nearly five years ago. Karen's friendly nature and ready smile makes anyone feel at ease from the moment they meet her. She's one of those women who, after you talk to her for just half an hour, you feel like you've been life-long friends. She has a gift of easily connecting with everyone she meets. This trait makes her perfect for the gig she currently has at a wine-tasting room, which is located just minutes from where she lives, allowing her the flexibility to be at home with her family as needed while enjoying sharing good wine and meeting new people each week.

*Day 11: What choice has had the greatest impact on your life?*

While we have all had different levels of social distancing comfort during the covid-19 pandemic, Karen describes herself as being incredibly cautious. When we met, restaurants in our area had just been allowed to open their inside seating from twenty-five to fifty percent. Because Karen had not yet received the covid-19 vaccine, she felt more comfortable sitting outside — which was perfectly fine with me. The one thing we didn't realize is that the outside heat lamps at the restaurant were not running. We ended up enjoying our conversation so much that we put aside any discomfort from the cold. Despite the lack of heat lamps and the rainy forty-degree weather, we managed to sit outdoors under a tent at the restaurant for three hours.

When Karen thinks back to the various choices she has made during her forty years of life, she says that one of the choices with the greatest impact in her life happened towards the end of her high school career, when she decided to pursue a four-year college degree. At the time she made the decision, she was not necessarily thinking about her future. She is a self-described "adapter" who until college lived in the shadow of her sister — who is twenty-two months older, popular, talented, and beautiful. Karen recalls her sister receiving much more of her parents' attention as they were being raised, simply because her sister's personality demanded more attention.

Karen subconsciously always seemed to know that she was the one who was expected to be okay — that she would figure things out on her own because she was known to simply adjust to survive any given situation, including her parents' divorce. Her grades in high school were mediocre, as getting high marks was not something she valued or prioritized. At some point, unknowingly, Karen settled into the role of simply being satisfactory and merely adapting to whatever came her way — not ever really planning for her next steps but rather reacting to what life brought her.

While in high school, she worked at Boston Market, a national chain restaurant. While working there, she met a co-worker who was planning on attending Western Washington University. Her co-worker's experience prompted Karen to consider for the first time the possibility of college. On somewhat of a whim, she took the SAT exam. To her surprise, she scored quite high. Her high score opened the door to several schools for her.

Her initial thought was that she would simply follow her co-worker and attend Western Washington University, but when she found out that the application process involved writing an essay, she chose to attend Washington State University (WSU) instead — a school whose admission process at the time did not include a required essay. It was not that Karen couldn't write an essay; she simply didn't feel like the effort was worth the payoff. Looking back now, she realizes that prior to attending college, her confidence in her own abilities and even her own worthiness was lacking.

When Karen entered WSU, all freshmen were required to take an assessment to determine their likelihood of succeeding in college. Based on the assessment, they were typically paired with an upper-class mentor. Karen scored so low on the assessment — results that basically said she was an at-risk freshman — she was then paired with a professor instead of a fellow student, to guide her through her first year.

Nevertheless, by her second semester, she surprised everyone, including herself. She was flourishing. Her grades were so impressive that she was invited to enter WSU's Honors Program. Once in the program, Karen continued to thrive. She realized for the first time that the world was her oyster. She was motivated to aim as high she could.

While visiting a friend's dorm room, she saw pamphlets for study abroad programs laid out in his living area. The pamphlets sparked a new interest and challenge. An essay was required as part of the application process, and this time she didn't hesitate to write one. She also needed three faculty recommendations to enter the exchange program. Her first recommendation came from her freshman advisor who had witnessed her transformation in college, and he was more than happy to give her a recommendation. Her second letter of recommendation came from a professor — someone Karen believes probably did not even know who she was due to the large size of the class — but he agreed to write a recommendation after he looked at his class records and saw that she'd scored the highest grade in the class. She can't recall who the third letter of recommendation came from, but undoubtedly given Karen's fabulous college performance, finding that third one was not difficult. Karen spent her entire junior year studying abroad in Scotland, which led to travel around Europe, where she acquired an international group of friends.

Choosing to attend college was the catalyst that began an amazing life journey for Karen — not only including study abroad, but also getting out of her sister's shadow. She met and made friends with a diverse group of people, gaining confidence in her abilities. And, perhaps most importantly, she lost the fear of speaking up — realizing that she no longer had to settle for being simply adaptable. She could take control and sit in the driver's seat of her life.

# Journal

*Today's date is:*

---

*Journal prompt: What choice has had the greatest impact on your life?*

---

---

---

---

---

---

---

---

---

---

---

---

---

---

---

---

---

# Day 12

## What did you dream about as a kid that you have made a reality?

Patti

Born: Arzu, Algeria

Headstone: It was a great run, and I wouldn't change a thing

Patti and I have known one another for years but have never carved out time to simply talk and get to know one another. Over the years, several of our mutual friends suggested that we get together because of the number of life experiences that we have in common. For starters, we are both international adoptees who have scant information about our adoption and the surrounding circumstances. As we discussed our adoptions, I mentioned that given where we came from, there were a lot of pieces that had to snap into place for the universe to bring us together.

*Day 12: What did you dream about as a kid that you have made a reality?*

It is funny when someone brings up a childhood memory that transports you back instantly to that moment in time.

Patti asked, "Do you remember the television show, *Mutual of Omaha's Wild Kingdom?*"

I instantly lit up and exclaimed that I used to watch that show with my parents. Patti remembers watching the show with her grandma, who was probably about the same age as my parents. Just to be sure I had the correct show in mind, I asked if the narrator was an older white-haired gentleman, and she smiled.

"Yes"! And there we were, transported back to childhood by the voice of Marlin Perkins.

One episode stood out to Patti, and it has had a lasting impact on her. She was eight years old, and the show was about cheetahs. They captivated her. Again, bringing up a childhood memory, she asked if I remembered using encyclopedias for book reports. I immediately recalled the *World Book Encyclopedia* and the *Encyclopedia Britannica*. I remember both being in the school library and getting excited when my parents purchased a set of *World Books* for our home. I recall my dad telling me that the purchase of a set of encyclopedias was an investment.

I used to sit on the floor of my childhood bedroom, reading through them — plagiarizing the pages for school reports. Not long after watching the *Wild Kingdom*'s episode on cheetahs, Patti wrote a book report, using an encyclopedia. The more she learned about the animal, which has been fighting extinction for decades, the more she knew she wanted to help them and other wildlife.

Initially, as a child, she dreamed of becoming a veterinarian, but as she got older — like many of us, myself included — she ignored her passion, and chose a career path that would be more profitable. She was incredibly successful in the career she chose;

however, her passion for animals never went away and continued to grow stronger.

As it turns out, her childhood dream to help animals, in particular wildlife, was not lost. Her career and those she met along the way became a conduit that allowed her to have the means to visit Africa several times — where she met conservationists. Her first trip to Africa occurred when she was in her early 30s, and it changed her life. Seeing the wild animals in person in their natural habitat and being educated by world-renowned experts in animal conservation led her to become involved at both a local and global level.

As a resident of Seattle, she joined the board of the Woodland Park Zoo in her mid-30s and served on the board for several years. Through her efforts, she has not only donated her own time and resources to raising money and making sure that the zoo is running at the highest level possible — the Woodland Park Zoo has the highest level of accreditation that a zoo can have — she has also brought other businesses and individuals on board to help in her efforts to preserve wildlife through education and fundraising.

Patti enlightened me during our conversation. I have had the good fortune of traveling to South Africa, where I enjoyed a safari with my family. But I found that upon returning home it was difficult for me to visit a zoo. I asked her how she could support zoos when she's travelled to Africa and seen animals in the wild. She reminded me that for most of the zoo attendees, this is their only opportunity to see these animals in person. Through our conversation, I learned that it has been shown that when zoo visitors are able to see animals in person, they are more likely to become involved and understand the need for wildlife preservation, because they have felt a personal connection to the animal. She also shared the different accreditation levels of zoos. Much of the work of zoos nowadays is in research and in ensuring that endangered animals do not become extinct. The research that is done is for the survival of a good number of species. Speaking to her changed my misguided view of zoos. Because of our conversation, I look forward to visiting and supporting the work of accredited zoos.

From the age of eight, her commitment to saving the animals has not wavered. Patti shows that you don't need to work directly in the area that was your passion as a child. There are other ways to feed your passion. My hope is that Patti's story sparks you to revisit your childhood passion — to find ways to refuel it and live the rest of your life filled with passion.

# Journal

*Today's date is:*

---

*Journal prompt: What did you dream about as a kid that you have made a reality?*

---

---

---

---

---

---

---

---

---

---

---

---

---

---

---

*Day 13*

# What's your definition of success?

Christine
Born: Seattle
Headstone: Don't cry because it's over, smile because it
happened

Christine and I live in the same small city, a city located about thirty minutes northeast of Seattle proper. Christine's children are much younger than mine — currently in fourth and sixth grades — while mine are in their early college years. Even though we're in much different places in our life as far as motherhood goes, we still find conversation easy. I felt that I connected with Christine from the first time I met her. I love her no-fluff, straight-to-the-point style of communicating. While initially she may seem on the quieter side, that first impression quickly changes as Christine begins to engage. She has a quick wit that can come unexpectedly. She has infused laughter into every conversation I've had with her.

*Day 13: What's your definition of success?*

Christine believes that the definition of success is being comfortable in your own skin. In other words, it's being comfortable with who you are. This definition of success is something that she came to believe as true after having children. The virtue is one of her guides as she raises her daughter and son.

Her mother used to tell her, "You can't make everyone happy, so at least make yourself happy with your choice!"

And, as a parent, Christine now sees the wisdom in her mom's words.

When Christine and her husband think about their children's future, they would love for them to attend a four-year university, recognizing that having a college degree can open doors. Christine also realizes that the university route is not for everyone, so when the time comes, it is important to her that should each of their children choose to attend a four-year school, it is because it is their own desire and the right fit for them — not because they feel parental and societal pressure to attend. When the time comes for these big decisions, Christine hopes that whatever route they choose, each child feels comfortable in their own skin.

My husband and I never thought to discuss what we think success will look like for our kids, but I think it's a great discussion for couples of young children to have. It is a discussion that can help guide couples as they raise their children together.

What I love about the questions asked throughout this book project, and the deep conversations they elicit, is that the lessons that emerge are often not what I expected. I wasn't expecting Christine's response to contain parenting wisdom — reminding parents to ask, "Are my children comfortable in their own skin?" She uses this question as a guide in parenting — to steer choices and decisions that will help children feel successful: comfortable in their own skin.

The last thing Christine ever wants to do is to raise children who make decisions because of others' wishes rather than deciding what is best for themselves. She wants her kids to know who they are — to be comfortable and confident. I shared with Christine that when I mentored young girls, I recall a school counselor telling the high school girls that if they choose a career based on what they perceived was expected of them, on a title, or on money, then they will find themselves unhappy and stuck. However, if they choose a career based on their passion, they will make enough money — because they will naturally be good at it; and more importantly, they will be happy. This experience happened during a time when I was still practicing law and driving to work each day with Gloria Gaynor's song *I Will Survive* as my morning theme song.

Christine's answer made me realize that defining success is a good question to ask — not just when it comes to parenting.

We should periodically ask ourselves, "Am I happy in my own skin? And if I'm not, then what can I do about it?"

Asking ourselves how we define success can be a catalyst to help us live our most authentic life.

# Journal

*Today's date is:*

-----------------------------------------------------------------

*Journal prompt: What's your definition of success?*

-----------------------------------------------------------------

-----------------------------------------------------------------

-----------------------------------------------------------------

-----------------------------------------------------------------

-----------------------------------------------------------------

-----------------------------------------------------------------

-----------------------------------------------------------------

-----------------------------------------------------------------

-----------------------------------------------------------------

-----------------------------------------------------------------

-----------------------------------------------------------------

-----------------------------------------------------------------

-----------------------------------------------------------------

"Success is relative. Joy is not."
— Shari Leid

# Ask Yourself This

## High School and College Years: Shari's Own Reflections

I. *Where in your life do you feel misunderstood?* There have been many times in my life when I have felt misunderstood. Similar to Mayumi (Day 8), my appearance has triggered ideas from others about who I am based on stereotypes. It used to really affect me when I thought I was being judged solely because I am visibly an Asian American woman. In fact, when I was younger, being misunderstood would make me physically ill. It would consume me. I would become angry and not present myself in the most flattering light. Fortunately, my reaction to being misunderstood has changed. I no longer grow upset or experience a physical response. I know that my intent is never to harm someone, which gives me comfort when I am misunderstood. I always welcome dialog, so if individuals who I feel have misunderstood me are not open to a conversation, then it is more about them than about me. I say a small prayer for them in my heart, wishing them well. I take a deep breath and move forward.

2.  *What career advice would you give your sixteen-year-old self?* By the time I was sixteen, I had already volunteered as a Candy Striper for a local hospital since I was twelve. I received my first paying job as a receptionist at a local hair salon. I enjoyed both work experiences, but when it came time for me to think about what I wanted to do as a career, I never thought about what made me happy and what I enjoyed. Instead, I based my career choice on what I thought sounded prestigious and what I believed would provide a high income.

    If I were to give career advice to my sixteen-year-old self, I would tell her that the career she chooses should align with her desires and natural talents. I would advise her to stay away from choosing a career based on what she thinks others will be impressed with — and to steer away from a path if she is headed down it simply because she thinks it will lead to making the most money. I would tell my sixteen-year-old self to discover what she is passionate about, because if she follows her passions, chances are she will be good at her job and she will make enough money. And most importantly, she will be happy.

3.  *If you could time-travel back to an earlier time in your life, where would you visit and what would you do?* For my entire life I've had questions about my beginnings. I was orphaned a few months after birth and found in a cardboard box in a parking lot in Seoul, Korea, abandoned with no identifying information. If I could travel back in time, I would travel back to my first year of life — and assuming I would have superpowers to possess the memory and senses that I do now — I would travel back

to form a conscious memory of my birth mother's face and my birth surroundings. I often think that I witnessed my birth family and their surroundings, including seeing my birth mom's face — if only I could access those newborn and infant experiences. But try as I might, they are beyond my consciousness.

4. *What choice has had the greatest impact on your life?* Getting married to my husband, Rory, at age twenty-seven. I couldn't ask for a better spouse. He has been my constant support and has never stopped me from trying new careers, bringing friends into our home, and seeking new adventures. We've travelled the world together and we have raised two wonderful children. Together, we have created a life that dreams are made of. It is hard to believe that we have been together for over half of our lives. We literally have grown up together and somehow we have managed to grow in our own separate ways while managing not to grow apart.

5. *What did you dream about as a kid that you have made a reality?* I never thought about this until asking Patti (Day 12) this question. When I realized that all my dreams have come true, I found myself filled with wonder. Truly, everything I have ever dreamed of has come true: financial stability; two kids who are thriving as young adults; two dogs; becoming an attorney; becoming a writer; becoming a fitness instructor; traveling the world; walking on a runway at a fashion show; speaking as an expert on network TV; being on the big screen; and the list goes on and on. I believe that when you want something, and you

work hard to get there, the Universe responds in kind and meets you halfway. Responding to this question has been an eye-opening revelation for me that has left me filled with indescribable gratitude and a strong belief in our power to make our dreams come true.

6.   *What is your definition of success?* Happiness without effort.

# Ask Yourself This

## Early Adult Years

*Day 14*

# Who's the best teacher you ever had?

Justina
Born: Redley Park, Pennsylvania
Headstone: Beloved

There are some people you are just meant to meet. Even when you cross paths for only a quick moment, that moment proves to be life-changing. Meeting Justina for just a few minutes at a girlfriend's birthday party was one of those meetings. Justina attended the party alone, and we shared a high-top table. We chatted for maybe twenty minutes and later that week became Facebook friends.

It was a few months following the party that I reached out to her and to a friend of mine from law school, asking if they were both still single and whether they would be open to meeting one another. I'm not sure what possessed me to reach out to the two of them at that moment in time — but amazingly enough, they fell madly in love right away, and they are now married. Justina's husband and I have been friends for years and I have never seen him as happy as he has been since meeting her. This story is a great reminder that you never know what a chance meeting might bring.

*Day 14: Who's the best teacher you ever had?*

Justina's *who* in response to my question is more of a *what*. Justina credits her divorce (which happened before I met her) as being her best teacher. The painful experience brought so many unexpected teaching moments. Through the struggles of her divorce journey, she learned about herself — especially her strengths — and she learned the power of friendship while receiving many acts of genuine kindness. She was able to not only move forward, but to thoroughly process what she learned and experienced, which resulted in a much more self-aware and confident version of herself.

Some marriages end by mutual agreement; Justina's wasn't one of those breakups. Justina did not see her divorce coming. She was blindsided. She had been married for fourteen years, with two young children, and they were entering what she assumed would be an exciting time in their lives. Her husband's company relocated the family to Shanghai, China. It was shortly after their move to China — while items from the States were still in route to their new home — that her world came crumbling down around her. Her husband was having an affair.

She remembers with clarity the day she learned of the affair. She had just surrendered her U.S. passport for review. In China, when you are a new resident, you are required to temporarily surrender your passport to the government so that they can conduct a background check. She spoke very little Chinese and was unsure how, or even if, she could retrieve her passport to return to the States.

Fortunately, the company her husband worked for provided a driver for all its U.S. employees. Justina described her driver as "a big, kind, panda bear." She was able to explain her situation to him, and without hesitation, he drove her to the government office where she had surrendered her passport. She watched as he argued with officials in Chinese and miraculously was able to retrieve her passport. His quick action on her behalf was one of her first experiences with kindness — but not her last — during her difficult divorce.

Another example of kindness was demonstrated in the beauty of a friendship that surpassed distance and time. The evening she learned of her husband's affair, she called upon a friend whom she hadn't spoken to in nearly a decade, not because they'd grown apart, but simply because life had been busy. This was no ordinary friendship. The girlfriend she called had been her best friend from grade school until the time they each went off to college. The instant she called, she felt loved; she was comforted by a bond that neither time nor distance had broken.

In addition to feeling the love from her friend on one of her most devastating days, the Universe reached out and enveloped her in a hug. Justina is a writer and story strategist (www.JustinaChen. com). Her book, *North of Beautiful*, is about a girl with a port wine stain on her face — and the book had just been released. On one of her most vulnerable days, that very evening, Justina received her first email from a teenage reader. The teenage fan reached out to let her know that reading her book made her feel beautiful for the first time.

Justina realized that the Universe was telling her she was going to be okay.

Justina moved back to the States as soon as she was able, with her young son and daughter in tow. Her eldest child began school, and she would later learn that her divorce was fodder for mom gossip at the small independent Seattle school where her son attended. Unbeknownst to her, she had friends who stepped in when the gossip started who quickly put an end to any wagging tongues.

As she described these acts of kindness, Justina had an expression on her face that showed the absolute appreciation that she still carries for the other mothers who stepped in to help keep her safe. These moms weren't close friends at the time, yet they provided another example of kindness she experienced during her divorce.

While she was establishing herself as a writer, Justina had the privilege of not worrying about how or when she would receive royalty checks because of her then husband's steady income. Unfortunately, once she realized she was divorcing, she needed a more reliable paycheck. She had been out of the standard workforce for over a decade and wasn't sure where to turn. Fortunately, she had maintained strong connections with her former colleagues. She contacted a friend at Microsoft — the place where she'd worked just prior to choosing to stay at home to raise her children — and very quickly her colleague connected her to a group at Microsoft. Soon she was back working there, almost as if she hadn't skipped a beat. Her former colleague's ready response to her inquiry and need was again another example of kindness she was shown during the difficult time of her divorce.

During the divorce process, she developed empathy for others going through a divorce who had chosen to be the stay-at-home parent — those who did not have a work history, experience, or resources and connections to get as quickly back on their feet as she had been able to do. Justina shared tips for stay-at-home parents, which rose out of what she'd learned were important as she ventured back out into a life as a divorced mom of two young children:

1.  Do something every year that scares you, to keep on edge. You don't want to become stagnant. If you keep this practice up, then when something unexpected comes your way, like an unplanned divorce, you'll know you can handle it because you've handled things that have frightened and challenged you before.

2.  Keep yourself relevant. Understand the latest technology. Keep yourself marketable – whether that means volunteering at your children's school, running an auction, or volunteering on a non-profit board. Always do something to continue to build your resume.

And Justina shared a third gem — a fun dating tip which helped her navigate the often very difficult experience of dating after divorce in your 40s. It's a challenge that Justina developed for herself, with the goal of getting to know her dates without the pressure of a second date. I personally think it is brilliant advice for dating in your 40s and beyond: She decided to go on twenty-one first dates in twenty-one days. She let each of her dates know her plan and advised them that they shouldn't expect a second date until she had completed her twenty-one-date challenge. Not only did she have fun getting to know each guy without feeling the pressures that a first date can bring, but she also noticed that men began approaching her — even in airports — to ask her out.

This was something she had never experienced until she changed her mindset about dating.

Incidentally, she married her twenty-second date, which is the one I happened to set her up on.

Justina experienced so much personal growth by going through her divorce. She is an Ivy League graduate, and a person who always did things by the book. She had prepared and planned what seemed like a picture-perfect life. But when life threw her a curve ball, it became her biggest teacher.

# Journal

*Today's date is:*

-----------------------------------------------------------------

*Journal prompt: Who's the best teacher you ever had?*

-----------------------------------------------------------------

-----------------------------------------------------------------

-----------------------------------------------------------------

-----------------------------------------------------------------

-----------------------------------------------------------------

-----------------------------------------------------------------

-----------------------------------------------------------------

-----------------------------------------------------------------

-----------------------------------------------------------------

-----------------------------------------------------------------

-----------------------------------------------------------------

-----------------------------------------------------------------

-----------------------------------------------------------------

-----------------------------------------------------------------

-----------------------------------------------------------------

When I feel overwhelmed
by work, it usually isn't
because I have too much
work to do, it is because
I'm doing work that doesn't
align with my soul.

# Day 15

## What piece of advice would you give your younger self if you could?

Stacey
Born: Lynwood, Washington
Headstone: Here lies a dedicated mother, loving friend, and
daughter, who did her best

Stacey and I met through a mutual girlfriend when I happened
to text this girlfriend one day and found out that she was
enjoying a gorgeous Pacific Northwest afternoon with friends at
a local wine-tasting venue, and she invited me to stop by. Stacey
was one of the friends enjoying the impromptu gathering. *Engaging,
kind,* and *beautiful* are the three words that come to mind when I
think about my first impression of Stacey.

*Day 15: What piece of advice would you give your younger self if you could?*

When asked what piece of advice she would give to her younger
self, Stacey's thoughts immediately went back to around age thirty,

when she worked in the tech industry. The firm where she worked was in a large high-rise in downtown Seattle known as "The box the Space Needle came in" — the tallest building in Seattle. Not only was her career demanding, but she was also juggling marriage and motherhood. When she thinks back to that time in her life, she recalls being constantly stressed. Her stress was so significant that it manifested itself physically. At night, she found that she was grinding her teeth while she slept, and during the day she was biting her nails. She was consciously and unconsciously damaging her health, happiness, and overall wellbeing. She was not only in a highly competitive workplace — and a male-dominated industry — she felt stuck.

Stacey's life now feels so much different from how it was when she was in her 30s, overwhelmed by stress. While she made several changes, including a move to a different career, the crux of the change happened through a difference in perspective. The shift in her perspective led her to landing in a place where she no longer felt stuck. But this did not happen overnight.

The transformation began to take place when Stacey read *Real Magic: Creating Miracles in Everyday Life* by Dr. Wayne W. Dyer. The book prompted deep self-reflection, which spurred a change in her mindset. Stacey slowly began to establish a habit of daily meditation. Nowadays sometimes she even meditates twice daily. She can feel it in her body on the days she skips her meditation practice.

The situation where she finds herself now — a place of inner peace and confidence — has resulted from her constant growth and movement, happening gradually over the past fifteen years. She now feels in control of her life and has a sense of both balance and wellbeing. She no longer feels stuck.

I'm not surprised to learn that Stacey feels good about where she is now. Her sense of wellbeing radiates when you see her. She believes in the power of health and healing through how she lives, what she eats, and how she moves. In addition to meditation, she incorporates a healthy lifestyle through nutrition and physical activity.

Without a doubt, if she could go back in time, she would show her younger self how to shift her perspective so that she would not stay long in that place of feeling stuck. She would tell her younger self to breathe and remind herself that she always has opportunity and choice. She would pull herself out of the rat race earlier than she did, despite the good money she was earning, because the toll it took on her overall wellbeing was not worth it. She would teach her younger self the power of meditation — how to quiet the mind.

I loved sitting down with Stacey and being reminded that seizing the power of choice, changing your perspective, and taking control of your life is a lesson that we can learn and incorporate at any age.

# Journal

*Today's date is:*

-------------------------------------------------------------------

*Journal prompt: What piece of advice would you give your younger self if you could?*

-------------------------------------------------------------------

-------------------------------------------------------------------

-------------------------------------------------------------------

-------------------------------------------------------------------

-------------------------------------------------------------------

-------------------------------------------------------------------

-------------------------------------------------------------------

-------------------------------------------------------------------

-------------------------------------------------------------------

-------------------------------------------------------------------

-------------------------------------------------------------------

-------------------------------------------------------------------

-------------------------------------------------------------------

-------------------------------------------------------------------

-------------------------------------------------------------------

"It's the journey that matters;
reaching the destination is simply
the icing on the cake."
— Shari Leid

# Day 16

## What's the best career compliment you've ever received?

LaShanda
Born: Montgomery, Alabama
Headstone: I can do all things through Christ who strengthens
me — Philippians 4:13

LaShanda and I met about ten years ago through a mutual friend who was one of LaShanda's co-workers at the time. When I met LaShanda she was working at a private school for sixth- to twelfth graders, which my son attended for both his middle-school and high-school years. While LaShanda was only at the school for a couple of his middle-school years, I loved running into her at the school during that time, greeted by her amazing energy and friendly smile. Her energy and smile light up a room.

*Day 16: What's the best career compliment you've ever received?*

LaShanda grew up in a military household. Her father was in the Air Force, so she spent her early years moving from place to place, until her fifth-grade year, when her family settled in the

Pacific Northwest. Despite being a gifted track athlete, LaShanda was teased for being the skinny girl. The experience of moving to different schools throughout grade school and the fact that she was teased often weighed heavily on her. These childhood incidents and hurt feelings chipped away at her self-esteem. She stopped running track her senior year of high school and decided to move directly into the workforce rather than go to college upon graduation.

LaShanda found success in the workplace but wasn't completely fulfilled. While working in a position she held for nine years, despite excelling at her job, she found that she was constantly told that she would never be promoted due to her lack of a college degree. Over those nine years, the comments concerning her lack of degree took away her confidence.

However, one day, LaShanda received the best career compliment — something which changed how she saw herself. Her work colleague told her that Lashanda's work ethic was one to be valued, and that their supervisors were not seeing the immense value she'd brought to the organization. She told LaShanda that it was time for her to move on, because her worth was being overlooked.

Hearing her co-worker's words sparked a flame that gave LaShanda the self-assurance, drive, and determination she needed to make things happen for herself. She realized that her worth did not come from a degree or lack of one, but from her own unique skills and hard work. Following this conversation, LaShanda began looking for jobs based on her work experience and talent, and she found a position with another employer that not only offered more responsibility and recognition, but also fed her desire to thrive — not just survive — at work.

While 2020 was a tough year for many, and LaShanda experienced her share of challenges due to the covid-19 pandemic, it was also a big year filled with successes for her. At age forty-five, after a lot of very hard work, she completed a goal that she'd set out for herself many years ago: She received her Bachelor of Arts degree in Business Administration. LaShanda is very proud of her accomplishment, and she is even prouder that she has set an example for her children — showing them that it is never too late to achieve your goals. She obtained her college degree because she wanted it for herself — not because she felt pressured by others to obtain it to prove her worth.

LaShanda is not only happier than ever but she is also much more confident. Once she let go of being directed by the fear of judgments from others, her self-reliance began to flourish.

The effect of LaShanda's colleague's compliment reminds me that words matter. You never know when your words can make an impact. Your words can give people the strength they need to move forward. It is because of experiences like Lashanda's that I see how important it is to have these deeper conversations.

# Journal

*Today's date is:*

------------------------------------------------

*Journal prompt: What's the best career compliment you've ever received?*

------------------------------------------------

------------------------------------------------

------------------------------------------------

------------------------------------------------

------------------------------------------------

------------------------------------------------

------------------------------------------------

------------------------------------------------

------------------------------------------------

------------------------------------------------

------------------------------------------------

------------------------------------------------

------------------------------------------------

------------------------------------------------

"You can change the world."
— Shari Leid

If you live for the *likes*,

you'll die by the criticism.

# *Day 17*

# How do you best receive criticism?

Cindy
Born: Bellevue, Washington
Headstone: She lived. She laughed. She loved.

Cindy and I live on opposite coasts: She's in South Carolina and I'm in Washington state. We met briefly in person years ago before she moved to the East coast. While we've been social media friends for a while, we've gotten to know each other much better over the last year through several Zoom calls.

*Day 17: How do you best receive criticism?*

Cindy co-owns several med-spas (www.backto30.com). She is not only business savvy, but she also has remarkable management skills. She is a natural problem-solver, and like my girlfriend Nicole (Day 34), Cindy would be one of my top five picks to make up a dream team for any project I'm involved in. She is not just a deep thinker and go-getter; she is also a go-doer. She gets things done. Because Cindy works with so many people — from business colleagues to employees to clients — I was not only curious to learn how she receives criticism but also how she delivers it to others.

Cindy began our conversation by reflecting back to her childhood, sharing how her response to criticism has shifted over time. She is the oldest of three children. She has a younger sister and brother, each of them about two years apart. Cindy describes her sister as the athletic one, especially gifted when it came to swimming, and her brother as the goof-off. He was always so fun-loving, with so much bright energy though, it was hard to ever be upset with him.

Her parents kept the kids active, and swimming was a big part of her childhood. All three kids were competitive swimmers. Even though swimming may not have been the first sport of choice for Cindy and her brother, it was easiest for her parents if all three were enrolled in the same sport. So, with her sister's natural gift for the sport, swimming became the family sport. The family travelled often to go to swim meets. Many of their weekends were spent at meets, which ran from early morning into the early evening hours.

It was these early competitive swimming experiences that she thought about when she reflected on how she once reacted to criticism. Her response as a child and as a teen was to rebel whenever she was criticized — not with yelling, but in a passive-aggressive manner. An example she shared came from a time when she switched from swimming to tennis. She recalls vividly her dad's attempts to coach her in tennis. She remembers him criticizing her swing, and in response she hit the ball purposely across several courts to make him run to retrieve the ball. At a young age, criticism motivated Cindy to fight back, to rebel against what was wanted from her. It was not the motivating tool that her coaches or her parents were hoping for.

Cindy's response to criticism changed as she got older. While a college student at Portland State University, Cindy was hired as a seasonal employee for Nordstrom in the fine jewelry department. Cindy was so skilled in sales that her seasonal position became a permanent position. She eventually became a Sales Associate in her favorite department at the store — the Savvy department — which showcased all the latest "it" designers, catering to the most stylish fashion-forward women in Portland, Oregon. Her clientele included many pro athletes' wives, and women who in today's world would be known as *influencers*. It was during her time at Nordstrom that she had a mentor whom she credits with teaching her not only about Sales but also about the importance of communication, understanding people, and learning how to give and take criticism in a way that is beneficial and helpful to everyone.

Her four years at Nordstrom gave Cindy the leadership tools that she still uses today. She learned that it is important to understand the people that you are working with. While at Nordstrom, Cindy kept a notebook, reminding herself of her clients' birthdays, and some of her clients' favorite things. She even made notes about what they shared regarding their families and friends — things that were important to them. She wrote down anything that helped her understand and communicate more successfully with her clients. In the same way, she learned how to converse effectively with co-workers and those whom she supervised. She credits both her mentor Sue and the Nordstrom family for these lessons.

At the time Cindy worked for Nordstrom, the Nordstrom family was involved in many of the day-to-day operations. She noticed that whenever there was an employee issue, Sue or the family would start the conversation with the employees by telling them everything they did right. They pointed out their strengths, so that when it came time to deliver the piece of criticism that needed to be shared, it was delivered with a focus on the benefit of improvement. The entire delivery was very positive, teaching her that criticism can be done constructively — in a completely healthy manner.

Cindy remembers another work-related experience, when she was working in Human Resources for another big fashion giant, Tommy Bahama. She received a glowing performance review that included the word *tactical* to describe how she managed her HR position. She immediately disliked the word and thought the word *strategic* was a more favorable-sounding word. When she suggested the word change, her supervisor explained that the word was being used as a compliment and she should take it as such.

As she thought about the word that was chosen in her review for a specific reason, she realized that it is not just the tone used and what is being said, but also the intent behind words that matters. This life lesson — taking into consideration the intent behind words and actions — has stayed with her, not only in professional settings as both an employer and an employee, but also in her personal life. It has helped broaden her perspective, allowing her to make better connections through the way she communicates.

Cindy now looks at criticism as a tool for improvement rather than something to fight against as she did when she was a child. In both her personal life and work life, she tries to remove herself from the initial emotion that criticism can bring. She takes a step back and breaks down the intent behind the words — so that she can either receive them or share them in a way that promotes a move forward in a positive direction.

Cindy closed our conversation with a great story — a lesson she learned from her husband who is a gifted Marketing Executive. As a Marketing professional, one of his favorite mottos is, "Don't let them see your buttons." In other words, don't let others see what buttons they can push that could get you easily riled up.

She realized early in their relationship that once she came to recognize someone's hot buttons, including his, it was easy in an argument to go right to those buttons. However, she found that it felt like she was "fighting dirty" — and she didn't like that feeling. She saw that this type of arguing slows down movement towards a resolution. She now tries to stay away from those hot buttons when offering criticism so that the criticism can be used as a constructive tool for moving forward.

# Journal

*Today's date is:*

-------------------------------------------------------------------

*Journal prompt: How do you best receive criticism?*

-------------------------------------------------------------------

-------------------------------------------------------------------

-------------------------------------------------------------------

-------------------------------------------------------------------

-------------------------------------------------------------------

-------------------------------------------------------------------

-------------------------------------------------------------------

-------------------------------------------------------------------

-------------------------------------------------------------------

-------------------------------------------------------------------

-------------------------------------------------------------------

-------------------------------------------------------------------

-------------------------------------------------------------------

-------------------------------------------------------------------

-------------------------------------------------------------------

"Smiles are contagious; spread that sh*t!"
— Shari Leid

# Day 18

## Would you rather be the worst player on a winning team or the best player on a losing team?

Lori
Born: Bridgeport, Connecticut
Headstone: Life's most rewarding journeys are the relationships
you choose to invest in.

It felt like a gift to meet with Lori in person for this conversation. In 2020, I joined the board of a local non-profit, where she was serving her final term as president. Because it was the year of social distancing due to the covid-19 pandemic, all our board meetings were held virtually. Our meeting was the first time seeing one another in person and not through a Zoom lens.

*Day 18: Would you rather be the worst player on a winning team or the best player on a losing team?*

Lori had an activity-filled childhood — she was in music competitions, she played on sports teams, and she was involved in a variety of extra-curricular groups. I imagine some of the early experiences in music and sports contributed to her strong work ethic and persistent drive. I also wouldn't be surprised if the experiences she had in team sports and group projects throughout her childhood and teenage years influenced her commitment towards supporting the success of her co-workers.

She is not 100 percent sure that the answer she has today to my question would have been her answer when she was younger; but today, she would rather be the best player on a losing team instead of the worst player on a winning team. It is not for the glory of being a superstar, or to feel superior. She'd rather be the best player on a losing team because she believes she would then have a greater opportunity to make a positive difference in her teammates' lives if she were in such a position.

I realized as we dove further into the discussion that Lori immediately viewed her place of "stardom" as an opportunity to move into a position of support for her teammates. As the best player, she would have the chance not only to develop leadership skills, but also to learn how to bring out her teammates' strengths, and how to keep them motivated.

And that is the mark of a good leader — using your position as a vehicle to lift your team up. Our discussion reminds me of what I often share with my mindset coaching clients: "The journey should feel like how you hope reaching the goal will feel."

Lori is a Human Resources professional, with years of experience in the field. She has dedicated her work life to managing people — addressing personnel issues, interpersonal issues, facilitating working relationships, and figuring out how best to support a work team. She recognizes that a team's sustainability is as strong as its weakest link. While she wouldn't describe herself as the "star" of the workplace — and definitely would not describe the employees she works with as a "losing team" — her role is one of support. She seeks to bring out the best in her team so that everyone's talents can support the team at large.

Speaking with Lori reminded me of a debate that I overheard my dad having with one of his colleagues back in the late 1970s. I was around eight years old, and I remember the debate so clearly. My dad was an instructor at Seattle Community College's Program for the Deaf. A discussion was being held regarding whether it was better for a student who was hard of hearing, and who had some language skills and/or could read lips, to attend a mainstream school or to attend a school for the deaf. I learned through listening to the debate, that more often than not, when hard-of-hearing students attended a mainstream school, they would often be left behind and perform at the bottom of the class; however, if those very same students attended the deaf school where they often had the highest set of language skills due to their less-significant hearing loss, then those students would blossom into leadership roles and become much more confident and happier adults.

Being the best player on the worst team can feel as good as winning that title, if you look for the wins along the journey.

# Journal

*Today's date is:*

-------------------------------------------------------------

*Journal prompt: Would you rather be the worst player on a winning team or the best player on a losing team?*

-------------------------------------------------------------

-------------------------------------------------------------

-------------------------------------------------------------

-------------------------------------------------------------

-------------------------------------------------------------

-------------------------------------------------------------

-------------------------------------------------------------

-------------------------------------------------------------

-------------------------------------------------------------

-------------------------------------------------------------

-------------------------------------------------------------

-------------------------------------------------------------

-------------------------------------------------------------

-------------------------------------------------------------

"Walk into a room with good energy and elevate your experience."
— Shari Leid

# Day 19

## Where are you not accepting that you're part of the problem?

Denise

Born: Seattle

Headstone (*Denise envisions this saying placed on a bench overlooking the water*): All who wander are not lost

Denise is the girl I've known all my life, yet never really knew. We are from the same neighborhood. I remember in grade school hearing about Denise and her brother before even meeting them. The neighborhood kids were in awe of the siblings' clear, bright green eyes. Both, mixed race, Black and White, residing in our primarily Black American and immigrant neighborhood, she and her brother stood out — because seeing Black children with bright green eyes was a rarity. I have a distinct memory of visiting the apartment complex where she and her brother lived. She was standing at the door, quietly talking to the friends I was with. I recall being intimidated by her. She seemed quiet, if not a little shy. She had an air about her when we were children that made her seem older than her age.

Day 19: *Where are you not accepting that you're part of the problem?*

Not too long before covid-19 brought many businesses to a screeching halt, Denise and her childhood friend, Darci, began a business together. It was Darci's brainchild, and she wanted Denise to join her as a business partner because they both have similar personal mission statements — to do what they can to uplift the Black American community. Denise took a long time to decide whether entering a business partnership was the right fit for her. She is a wanderer, an explorer by nature — a woman who has never liked to feel tied down. Running a business initially felt constraining.

However, the business idea that Darci presented to her was one that she couldn't walk away from. It wasn't just the potential money that could be made, but it was the mission that she couldn't let go of. She meditated on it and thought about it for weeks before committing. It was a social-media photo that made her realize that she couldn't turn away. The photo was of a Black man's wrists in shackles.

Her impulse for starting the business — along with her partner's motivation — is to lift people up, to give second chances, to help people who often through no fault of their own have been placed in a compromising position. It could be a former military veteran, someone who grew up on welfare, or a person who has rehabilitated after serving time in prison — individuals from the community who simply want an honest job, not a handout. Denise and Darci together formed a company they called Alltrus (www.alltrus.com), which is now a trusted leader in the cleaning business. Their mission statement is to provide superior service and sustainable solutions that support the planet and provide opportunities that positively impact economic growth to build up and enrich communities.

Once they began the commercial cleaning business, they were off to a great start. But when the pandemic hit, their cleaning business came to an abrupt halt as they tried to navigate the ever-changing protocols. Trying to keep business going and balancing the needs of their workers for safety, combined with the stress and requirements of their clients, was a big challenge. There were times when she knew in her gut that they were being taken advantage of by a few clients. And she didn't speak up. This was when she realized that she had been part of the problem. Failing to speak up and stand her ground was costing her business money, causing her unneeded stress, and requiring her to do more work than what she was being compensated for. While she could point a finger at the businesses who took advantage of the situation, took advantage of her employees, or even took advantage of her and her business partner — she instead took ownership of the situation — looking at her own actions and what she could do to move business forward.

Upon reflection, she realized she was taking on more than she needed to. Even after hiring an Executive Director, Denise was not letting go of many of the tasks that the Director was hired to do. She began to recognize that some of the things in her business that she was not happy with were happening because she was part of the problem. At the time we spoke, Denise was planning on taking her first vacation in months. Recognizing how she was part of the problem — in instances where the business lost money and where she and her partner were taking on more day-to-day tasks than necessary — this realization has been the game changer.

Denise's story reminds me that when things aren't going well and we place the blame on someone else without looking at ourselves first, we give our power away. When we don't take responsibility, we feel stuck — which keeps us from moving forward and seeing opportunity. When Denise was able to see how she was holding herself and her business back from being as successful as she hoped it could be, she was finally able to see opportunity and choice — to make the situation better.

I'm inspired by Denise's constant desire to grow and learn. And speaking to her reminds me that this is really a question we should ask ourselves often: Where in my life am I not accepting that I'm part of the problem?

# Journal

*Today's date is:*

_____

*Journal prompt: Where are you not accepting that you're part of the problem?*

_____

_____

_____

_____

_____

_____

_____

_____

_____

_____

_____

_____

_____

_____

# Day 20

## What life lesson took you more than once to learn?

Angela
Born: San Pedro, California
Headstone: She was a good ancestor

I met Angela at my father-in-law's celebration of life service. As a former student of my father-in-law, who was a professor at Washington State University (WSU), she was asked by the family to speak about the memories she had of him and the positive impact he'd had in her life. It was clear from her speech that he had made a profound impact while she was an undergraduate. She eloquently took the event attendees back to the late 1980s and early 1990s, when she attended WSU. Her stories made the audience both laugh and cry — including when she shared the angst she experienced as a young Blasian woman moving to an area of the state and a school not known for its racial diversity. Through her stories, we not only felt the impact of the bond between a professor and a student; we also glimpsed the beginnings of the emerging leader that Angela is now.

*Day 20: What life lesson took you more than once to learn?*

Angela and I were destined to meet. As it happens, twenty-seven years ago at my first job out of law school, I worked with Angela's former college roommate. Not only that, she and my former co-worker lived in my husband's family home, while students at WSU, when his parents were on sabbatical in the Netherlands. Angela and I have also noticed through social media that we have several mutual friends. It always feels a little bit like "coming home" when someone walks into your life, and you know you were supposed to meet.

Upon graduation from WSU, Angela moved directly into a leadership position, becoming a Director — supervising mostly Caucasian women who were often twice her age. From that, she moved into another Director position, then to a Chief of Staff position, followed by a Vice President position; and before long she became a CEO. She constantly moved into positions of leadership, often supervising people who were much older than she was. Her goal out of college was to get to that next level of leadership, so she was always chasing titles.

Looking back at her thirty-plus-year career, Angela knows that during her first three positions of leadership, she led by treating everyone the same — focusing on their job roles and titles more than on who they were as individuals. During this time, she was also juggling her career — she was a mom and trying to figure out how best to parent and support her children. Always open to learning, and wanting to do better, she began to modify the way she not only led but also how she parented — realizing that just as her children each have different personalities and talents, so do her employees.

Both her leadership and parenting styles began to change. This lesson in leadership wasn't learned overnight — and she admits that it took her more than once to learn.

She made it her mission to get to really know and understand each person she supervised. She focused on how to empower each person by recognizing individual skills and talents. She developed a leadership training program for her staff, which not only supported them in their current roles but also gave them a skill set to help them advance their careers, even if that meant that at some point, she would likely lose them.

In this process, she became an authentic leader. She became open and honest with her employees, including sharing when she had a task to accomplish that she felt could be better handled by an employee. An example happened in 2021, during an onslaught of Asian hate — a fall-out from the coronavirus pandemic. One morning before work, she saw disturbing news footage of an older Asian woman being attacked. The news hit her at her core — she felt palpable fear for her mother's safety — and her heart and mind felt heavy. In years past, she would have forged through work. This time, however — having trust in her team — she told them that she was struggling that day with something personal, and that she trusted them to step in and fill her shoes. Her authenticity in demonstrating trust in her team strengthened the bonds between team members. She was leading by example.

During the pandemic, she wrote four words down: *Kind, Joy, Grace,* and *Love.* These four words became her guideposts for the way she planned to lead and the way she intends to live her life going forward. You can be firm, you can even take care of a disciplinary problem — and you can do it with kindness, joy, grace, and love. Angela's faith is important to her. She takes to heart what her mom taught her: "No matter your title, let them see Jesus in you."

The difference she witnessed in her employees after she became an authentic leader — a woman who looks at each employee as an individual and sees her biggest job as supporting and fostering growth — was monumental. She recently was recruited to a new job, and she decided to take the position because she saw how it provided an even greater opportunity for her to make an impact — not only with her employees but with her community at large.

# Journal

*Today's date is:*

---

*Journal prompt: What life lesson took you more than once to learn?*

---

---

---

---

---

---

---

---

---

---

---

---

---

---

# Day 21

## Which trip changed your life for the better?

Diane
Born: Detroit, Michigan
Headstone: She loved life and it loved her back

One of the words that I'd use to describe Diane, if I were to describe her appearance to someone who had not yet met her, is *fashionista*. She is a beautiful, stylish Greek American woman who was born and raised in Detroit, Michigan. She has the appearance and energy of a woman twenty years younger than her sixty years of age. She is proud of both her Greek roots and her Detroit grit. We initially met about three years ago when we participated in a local fundraiser that supported our region's medical emergency system. While there were several women involved in the local fundraiser, Diane stood out to me because she presented herself with the fabulous combination of confidence, kindness, and grace — which made her not only memorable, but also very welcoming and approachable.

Day 21: *Which trip changed your life for the better?*

Diane is the CEO and founder of PhotoPad for Business (www.photopad.co/). She has a background in social work, a career she was very successful at for over twenty-five years. She imagines that she would have stayed in social work — and perhaps even be ready to retire by this point — had she not taken the trip that changed her life.

The trip that changed her life is the move that brought her to Washington state, where she has resided with her husband since the late 1990s. It was a big move for Diane in part because until that point, she had never lived more than three hours away from her close-knit Detroit family. When she left for college, she attended school just thirty miles outside of Detroit, at Eastern Michigan. While the move to Washington state was prompted by her husband's career opportunity — to work for Microsoft — she could not have imagined in her wildest dreams that the move which pulled her out of her safe and secure environment would lead her to a successful career as an entrepreneur in the very male-dominated tech world.

About a year after moving to Washington state, she and her husband welcomed their son. Diane chose to stay home for a while, returning to social work as a consultant when her son was three years old, designing a schedule that would accommodate the work/life balance that she desired. During this time, she experienced travel, something she did little of until that point. To capture these amazing travel experiences, she started putting together digital albums — photos that told a story. She was talented at producing stories told through photos — this was during the pre–social media era — and her friends took notice and raved over the created albums. Diane's own hobby sparked her creative mind. She saw a need for an easy system to tell stories through photos. And that's when her life as an entrepreneur began.

Her company, PhotoPad for Business, has continued to evolve — since technology, social media, and digital marketing are in constant flux. Her mission is to help small businesses tell their stories through easy-to-manage templates, connecting to their customers through stories.

Her experience as an entrepreneur has meant that she's had to step outside of her comfort zone several times since the launch of her business — including pitching to investors; conducting live interviews with business leaders, community leaders, and influencers on social media; and much more. It is Diane's personal relationship with her clients and her commitment to understanding each client's individual needs that keeps her client list growing and increases her impact in the business community. Her amazing life experiences as a successful entrepreneur would never have happened had she stayed in her comfort zone near her hometown of Detroit and not taken that trip that changed her life forever.

Diane is a testament to the value of trusting yourself and getting out of your comfort zone. Just as a bird needs to leave the nest to fly, and a butterfly needs to escape its cocoon to soar, it's time for you to take that trip that will change your life.

# Journal

*Today's date is:*

-------------------------------------------------------------------

*Journal prompt: Which trip changed your life for the better?*

-------------------------------------------------------------------

-------------------------------------------------------------------

-------------------------------------------------------------------

-------------------------------------------------------------------

-------------------------------------------------------------------

-------------------------------------------------------------------

-------------------------------------------------------------------

-------------------------------------------------------------------

-------------------------------------------------------------------

-------------------------------------------------------------------

-------------------------------------------------------------------

-------------------------------------------------------------------

-------------------------------------------------------------------

-------------------------------------------------------------------

"Every new place I visit changes my life, my perspective and makes the world a little smaller."
— Shari Leid

# Day 22

## Other than financial rewards, what else have you gained in your current work?

Veronica
Born: Bremerton, Washington
Headstone: She laughed loudly, lived well, and loved deeply

Veronica and I met through a mutual friend. Over the past few years, we've had the opportunity to get together through our friend — who is a great connector, a social butterfly, and a successful entrepreneur. It is not surprising that my introduction to Veronica came from a very accomplished and driven woman, because that is also how I describe Veronica. She is the first in her family to graduate from college — and she did not stop there. After receiving her undergrad degree, she was accepted and enrolled into law school. She is now a member of the judiciary, serving as a Superior Court Judge for the largest county in Washington state.

*Day 22: Other than financial rewards, what else have you gained in your current work?*

We laughed at the way the question posed begins, "Other than financial rewards," because we are both very aware that lawyers do not become Judges to make the big money. In fact, other than the Public Defenders and maybe some of the Prosecutors, the Judge is often the attorney in the courtroom who is being paid the least. To serve on the bench truly involves a love for the law and a belief in the legal process. Judges have the potential of reaping much greater financial rewards if they choose private practice rather than dedicating themselves to public service.

Veronica recalls that from a young age, she carried a strong belief in the virtue of justice. Her initial introduction to the legal system was wrought with chaos. She describes her father as "legally challenged." It took me a second to realize what she was saying, and I started laughing at the political correctness contained in her choice of words. What she was saying is that her dad found himself in trouble with the law on more than one occasion. His troubles eventually led to his deportation to Mexico, leaving her mom to care for her young family alone.

I wondered, given what seemed to me to be a traumatic introduction to the legal system, why Veronica would choose to become part of something that resulted in her family being torn apart. She explained that she always had a strong sense of empathy — with the ability to see things from all sides. Even at a young age, she understood her father's role in the system, and although sometimes she may not have agreed with the way things were handled, she recognized the reasons the justice system was in place.

Veronica's mother was only nineteen years old when Veronica was born. Veronica is the oldest of three, with her two younger siblings several years her junior. Her mom's youth and the large age gap between her and her younger siblings brought on a lot of family responsibility at a very young age. Veronica was put into a situation where often, especially as she moved into her middle-school years, she acted and felt more like her mother's sister and her siblings' mother.

Veronica explained that in Mexican culture, family is very important — so family members are expected to contribute to the family's wellbeing above all else. When she chose to attend college, it felt like a selfish thing that she was doing — getting an education for herself and using most of her wages to pay for her tuition and books rather than sharing those earnings with her family.

Veronica managed to contribute to the family whenever she could, including purchasing a washer and dryer for her mom — an incredibly large expense for a college student making it on her own. After receiving her Bachelor of Arts degree in Sociology, she took a year off between college and law school, which gave her the ability to help her family financially a little more. During that gap year, in addition to saving up for law school expenses, she managed to earn enough money to help her mom purchase a home.

When she entered law school at the University of Washington School of Law, she and the other law students were advised not to work during their law-school careers — unless they were working as "Rule 9s," i.e., legal interns, during their final year of law school. Accordingly, most of her classmates did not work during their first year.

But Veronica did not have the luxury of not working. She worked as a cocktail waitress through her first and second years of law school, until she received a Rule 9 internship during her third year. The University of Washington only offered a daytime program, so she waitressed in the evenings — sometimes not getting off work until after 2:00 AM. Not only did her schedule pose challenges when it came to taking the classes, but it also kept her from being able to bond with her fellow classmates, which included joining study groups and going on social outings.

Veronica easily cites several times prior to taking the bench when she felt that justice wasn't being served — even dating back to her pre–law school years. She shared a couple of examples with me. Knowing from even before she began college that her goal was to become an attorney, she took a job while an undergrad as an investigator for a Public Defender's office. She recalls one case where she was required to question a victim of a sexual assault. Her job, being on the defense side, was to poke holes or find inconsistencies in the victim's story that could be used during the trial. The victim had been so traumatized by the assault that Veronica had to question her at the victim's own home because she was too afraid to leave her house. During the interview, Veronica realized that her questioning seemed to be further traumatizing the victim. While understanding the importance of her role as an investigator for the defense, she decided that she would obtain the information she needed — yet she wasn't going to be a part of further victimizing another human being. She chose to proceed with her investigation with compassion and never intimidation.

Another story that Veronica shared happened when she worked as a Prosecutor. During a trial over which she was prevailing, a recess was called. During the break, she went into the ladies' room and overheard two of the prosecution's witnesses celebrating the fact that they had "pulled one over" on everyone. She immediately returned to the courtroom and reported what she had heard to the Defense Attorney and the Judge, and asked for a dismissal of the case. It doesn't matter what side of the law Veronica is on, she is always fighting for justice — and keeping the integrity of the law intact.

What Veronica gains from her job and what she loves is being able to do research to fully understand the issues presented in cases and the precedents that may exist. When briefs are presented to her by attorneys, she reads the briefs, looks at the citations, reads the cases, and becomes fully informed on the law and the arguments. The deep dive into studying the law is a luxury that she never had the time to do while in law school, because she was working in the evenings and attending classes during the day.

While the justice system is not perfect, she has faith in it. She explained that the way to destroy a country is to destroy its justice system. That is how profoundly important our justice system is.

# Journal

Today's date is:

----------------------------------------

Journal prompt: Other than financial rewards, what else have you gained in your current work?

----------------------------------------

----------------------------------------

----------------------------------------

----------------------------------------

----------------------------------------

----------------------------------------

----------------------------------------

----------------------------------------

----------------------------------------

----------------------------------------

----------------------------------------

----------------------------------------

----------------------------------------

----------------------------------------

"Life is the best classroom that
I've ever been in."
—Shari Leid

# Day 23

## If all jobs paid the same, what would you choose to do?

Sarah
Born: Seattle
Headstone: She operated with love

As with many of my friendships, I met Sarah through a mutual friend. We met at that friend's annual Christmas Open House party. Sarah is one of the easiest people I know to talk to. I love her insights on life. She can comfortably communicate with everyone she meets. She is fiercely intelligent. She was salutatorian of her high school class and received her degree from Stanford in Mechanical Engineering and Product Design, working in a field that is still dominated by men.

*Day 23: If all jobs paid the same, what would you choose to do?*

At the time I met with Sarah, she had been at her job for just under a year. She was hired during the pandemic and had worked remotely from day one. She laughed as she explained that despite coming up on a year in the position, she had yet to meet her work team in person or to pick up a building worksite key badge. We commented on what an interesting time we live in. In fact, Sarah started the conversation by sharing the fact that 2020 was a year of self-reflection for her.

She immediately had an answer to my question: She said she has thought about this a lot over the past couple of years. She explained that she was in the process of forming a Limited Liability Company (LLC) whose mission would meet her passion. Sarah believes that everyone can make a difference through small acts of kindness each day. In the upcoming year, she plans to focus on building her legacy.

The LLC she is forming is exactly where she would invest all her time as her job — if it paid what she is currently earning. Sarah is a natural connector. She has worked with youth in a variety of capacities. Her work in the tech industry — the Mechanical Engineering and Product Design field — is an industry that still has very few women in it, let alone women of color. For many years, Sarah has recognized a gap in communication between industry needs and the work of non-profits worldwide. She knows that there are many non-profits doing great work that could benefit from her skills of connecting them to a place of need or even to other non-profits, to complement one another. She also connects sought-after talent to tech companies.

She loves mentoring young people, especially those from underserved communities. A gifted presenter, she is often asked to speak at events and to serve on speaker panels. When she is given an opportunity to present in front of an audience, to share her experience and expertise, if she thinks it is an opportunity that can benefit younger professionals, she'll often suggest they speak instead of herself, mentoring them from the sidelines.

Sarah has formed three pillars that define the goals and purpose for her LLC: Youth "Copowerment" — mutual challenge and collaborative perspective-shaping — Education, and Technology. She believes that if you guide yourself by your morals and your purpose, then you can't go wrong. Fortunately for her, even in her current job, much of what she does also aligns with her three pillars. She has used these pillars not only as a foundation for her LLC's mission statement, but also in her personal life to determine where she is going to spend her energy.

After speaking with Sarah, I am going to think about what my three principal pillars are, write those down, and pin them to my office bulletin board where they are easy to see.

I hope one day Sarah can dive 100 percent into her passion and live her dream job. While having raised her son on her own, although newly married, she is as of this writing realistically unable to quit her day job. But she is proof positive that you can have your cake and eat it, too. It's a reminder that we can nourish our soul and our dreams through projects in addition to our employment. Just because we can't quit our day job (yet), doesn't mean we can't also pursue our dream job. Life doesn't have to be all or nothing.

# Journal

*Today's date is:*

------------------------------------------------

*Journal prompt: If all jobs paid the same, what would you choose to do?*

------------------------------------------------

------------------------------------------------

------------------------------------------------

------------------------------------------------

------------------------------------------------

------------------------------------------------

------------------------------------------------

------------------------------------------------

------------------------------------------------

------------------------------------------------

------------------------------------------------

------------------------------------------------

------------------------------------------------

"It is not a job — it is my purpose, passion, and joy."
— Shari Leid

# Day 24

## Who was the best boss you ever worked for?

Sadie

Born: Havana, Cuba

Headstone: Live life in full gratitude

Sadie and I met five years ago at a girlfriend's birthday celebration. Sadie had been our girlfriend's work supervisor, and they have maintained a friendship for nearly two decades since they both left that place of employment. Sadie happens to live in a neighborhood that is just across the street from me. While she is a neighbor and friend, I never knew until this book project that she is also an end-of-life doula and inspirational coach (www.joyovergrief.com). This thrills me because I imagine that Sadie is incredibly gifted in this area. I am delighted that her journey has brought her to such an impactful career.

*Day 24: Who was the best boss you ever worked for?*

As Sadie started to describe the best boss she ever had, her face lit up, filled with obvious admiration. Sadie is a former practicing nurse. She found that being a bedside nurse was emotionally taxing because she cared so deeply for her patients. She subsequently moved into the business administrative side of nursing — and that is where she met Karen, the best boss she ever worked for. She described Karen as "an incredible person." Karen had the ability to lead effectively while also showing great compassion for her team members.

On Mondays, it was common for Karen to ask her employees if they had a good weekend. She'd ask them to share one great thing and one not-so-great thing about their weekend or their week. When the not-so-great experience was shared, Karen would ask if they could point to something good that came out of that experience. If the employee couldn't come up with anything that felt positive about the experience, she would invite that person to lunch and help to process the experience further. Karen was perhaps — without realizing it — the world's first mindset career coach!

Karen created a team environment. When AOL Messenger was relatively new, she made sure the entire team had AOL Messenger open on their computers so that they could easily communicate with one another throughout the day. She showed her employees how to make vision boards — not only for envisioning what they wanted their professional life to look like, but also what they wanted their entire life to look like. She taught her employees that they have control over their lives along with the ability to create their dream lives. When Karen saw that an action needed to be corrected, she would show not only how correcting the employee's action would benefit the entire team, but also how it would personally benefit the employee. Karen's focus was not simply on creating a healthy and productive environment but also on fostering happy, skilled employees.

Chances are that Karen does not know how much of an impact she has had because of her exceptional leadership skills. She not only helped her employees in their work and in their individual professional development; she also provided skills that transferred to their home life, influencing the way they parented their own children.

Sadie eventually left California and moved to Washington state, where she was a supervisor at a large hospital. There, she adopted many of the skills she'd learned from Karen.

In fact, because I was curious and had an idea of what her answer would be, I asked our mutual friend, Tee-Ta — the person responsible for bringing Sadie and me together — "Who is the best boss you ever had?"

And immediately she said, "Sadie." Tee-Ta described Sadie as the boss who helped her recognize her strengths and talents, fostered them, and supported her as she moved forward in her career. Tee-Ta said that Sadie was the boss with such a high level of emotional intelligence, she was not only a joy to work for, but she also made a positive and profound difference in her entire life.

Sadie is a living testament of how much of an impact a superb boss can have — not only directly upon their employees but in the world at large.

# Journal

*Today's date is:*

------------------------------------------------------------

*Journal prompt:* *Who was the best boss you ever worked for?*

------------------------------------------------------------

------------------------------------------------------------

------------------------------------------------------------

------------------------------------------------------------

------------------------------------------------------------

------------------------------------------------------------

------------------------------------------------------------

------------------------------------------------------------

------------------------------------------------------------

------------------------------------------------------------

------------------------------------------------------------

------------------------------------------------------------

------------------------------------------------------------

------------------------------------------------------------

------------------------------------------------------------

"The best boss is one that
leads future bosses."
— Shari Leid

# Ask Yourself This

## Early Adult Years:
## Shari's Own Reflections

1. *Who's the best teacher you ever had?* I'm blessed to be able to say without hesitation that my best teacher was my dad. He collapsed and died suddenly just a month after my thirty-second birthday. I am blessed to have had over thirty years of being raised by the best teacher I ever had. One of the greatest things he ever taught me was how to be a friend to everyone I meet.

2. *What piece of advice would you give your younger self if you could?* Being adopted — at a time when international adoptions or adoptions in general were not celebrated and talked about as they commonly are today — was not easy. As a Korean adoptee, adopted into a Japanese American family, I always felt that I wasn't fully accepted by many of my extended relatives who didn't hesitate to speak poorly of Koreans within my earshot. My parents also attended a Japanese American church, where I was the only Korean member until my teenage years, when a family of a Korean and Japanese mixed marriage began

attending. Even then, I remember members of the church pointing out that the husband was Korean and not Japanese. If there was one piece of advice I would share with my younger self, it is: "You belong."

3. *What's the best career compliment you ever received?* When one of my coaching clients, a woman in her mid-50s, said to me, "You have changed my life." I absolutely love coaching. Each time a client has a breakthrough that helps her to enjoy life to the fullest, my heart sings.

4. *How do you best receive criticism?* I've noticed that as I have gotten older, criticism does not affect me like it once did. Receiving criticism used to distress me to the point that I would become so angry that I felt physically ill. I would often strike back at the person who delivered the criticism. With age and experience, I've come to understand that criticism says more about the person who is doing the criticizing than it does about me. Receiving criticism is an invitation to learn about myself, about a skill, or even about the person doing the criticizing.

   When I've been able to reframe criticism as an opportunity rather than a confrontation, I've been able to use it to my advantage. Criticism can still initially sting and take the wind out of my sails when it first hits; therefore, I receive criticism best when it is sandwiched between nice words.

5. *Would you rather be the worst player on a winning team or the best player on a losing team?* I'm going to answer this question in terms of athletics. I'm not particularly athletically gifted. I have been one of the

worst players on a winning team in my youth, and it wasn't fun. Being the worst player on a winning team can chip away at self-esteem, and it doesn't feel good. Therefore, when it comes to athletic endeavors, I would rather be the best player on a losing team and be the leader — someone who can build the morale of my team and lift the self-esteem of my fellow players.

This becomes a harder question for me to answer if I think of work and business teams. Ideally, I would love to be on a team with equal contributors. But that is not what the question is asking. I gravitate towards leadership roles, but I sure wouldn't be effective if I were the best player of a working team that was not meeting its goals and seen as the worst among its peers. Therefore, I would rather be the worst player on a winning team — when it comes to work or business. It is interesting to think about how different my answers are when I consider this question in different settings.

6. *Where are you not accepting that you're part of the problem?* It is hard for me to accept that I am a part of the problem in relationships that aren't working as I wish they would. I think about my strained relationship with my mother. We don't argue or fight and I help her when I can; but we are very formal with each other. When I was a younger adult, I blamed her for the poor quality of our relationship because my view at the time was that if there is a bad relationship between a child and parent, it is the parent's fault. Children naturally want to be loved by their parents and make their parents happy.

While I still believe that parents hold the primary responsibility for the relationship that is cultivated with their children, I no longer believe that this situation can't shift. Sometimes these relationships can fail due to the failings of the child. It is hard for me to accept that I'm part of the problem when relationships aren't thriving, or even when friendships end — but I know I play a large role. I have actively worked on diverting my focus from blame to looking at myself — so that I can learn from relationships that have become strained or broken. I know I can do better in the future.

7. *What life lesson took you more than once to learn?* It took me a long time to realize that *I belong.* I wasted so much of my youth and young adult life trying to prove that I belonged — whether it was in my adoptive family, at my childhood church, in law school, in my career, or even in my mixed-race marriage. It wasn't until my 40s that I came into my own and really believed that wherever I am, I belong. I can't point to the exact moment of realization, but I think social media may have helped in my discovery. Social media gave me a platform to connect with a lot of different people and allowed me to be witty, angry, and happy in what started out as a safe place. I'll admit I was an over-sharer, so I've pulled back some on social media as it has grown, and I have matured. (Yes, you can continue to mature. It is never too late!) Yet I can't deny the positive effects social media has had on my life. Social media contributed to my understanding that no matter where I am, I belong.

8. *Which trip changed your life for the better?* The trip that was life-changing for me was traveling with my family to China, my

daughter's birth country. It gave me so much joy to see her take in the beauty of the land, the people, and the food of her birth country. I also witnessed parks in China filled with families who were happy — people enjoying life with children and grandparents. Viewing the joy and laughter of the Chinese people who lived in government housing in Beijing, many in small apartments, taught me that happiness is found in the relationships you have with family, friends, and community — not in worldly possessions or job titles.

We were also fortunate to travel throughout the vast country of China, far away from Beijing, seeing many different provinces. I learned through traveling in that country how my view of China (and of other places around the world) had been so limited by what I was shown on television or what I grew up understanding in school. There is no cookie-cutter description for a country or its people. The trip helped me feel a deep connection to all of humanity.

9. *Other than financial rewards, what else have you gained in your current work?* I joke with my husband that it always costs us money for me to work! The expenses incurred from running your own business can often be more than the actual income. But financial reward is the last thing motivating me to work as a coach and writer. What I have gained is the joy of waking up each morning knowing that I am making a difference in this world. I say a prayer of gratitude every morning. I have a career that I don't want to take a vacation from, which is a first for me! I'm so glad I finally found it in my late 40s. And it took off after age fifty!

10. *If all jobs paid the same, what would you choose to do?* Happily, I would do what I'm doing now: writing, life-coaching, and teaching!

11. *Who was the best boss you ever worked for?* In the early to mid-1980s, I volunteered as a Candy Striper at a Seattle-area hospital. I was twelve years old when I started volunteering, working full days during the Summer months. I was given a lot of responsibility — including charting patients' vitals — and I received constant praise from the nurses on the floor. I still remember one of my favorite nurse's names — Digene — who I learned so much from by simply watching the way she led. Her actions taught me to teach and lead with kindness — an example I've carried with me throughout my career. The nurses never talked down to me or treated me as if I were below them, even though I was just a kid volunteer. It was my first experience in the workforce, and having such amazing bosses established the strong base for my future success.

# Ask Yourself This

## Adulting

# Day 25

## List the five people you spend the most time with. How have they affected your behaviors, thoughts, and life?

Vivian
Born: Taipei, Taiwan
Headstone: Here lies a perpetual adventurer

When you think of Seattle events, you think of Vivian. She is Seattle's premier event photographer (www. vivianhsuphotography.com). I met Vivian about fifteen years ago, attending some of the Seattle area's larger events. While I always admired her, especially her style — which includes her own designed and handmade gowns — I really began to appreciate the way she lives life when I started following her Instagram feed. Quieter in nature, Vivian doesn't share her life through speech or writing but through her photos — which capture not just the beauty of her life but also the brilliance of the way she witnesses the world.

*Day 25: List the five people you spend the most time with. How have they affected your behaviors, thoughts, and life?*

The five people Vivian spends the most time with are friends she has known for over a decade. As she described these five friends to me — people I have never met — I felt like I was meeting them in person because of her vivid descriptions. The admiration and love she has for each of these friends was evident. It was important to her to properly convey the significance they hold in her life.

Vivian met her friend Nikki through Nikki's dad, who managed the photography studio where Vivian received her first professional photography job. Nikki's parents and brother treated her like family. In fact, soon after meeting Nikki, she began referring to her as her younger sister. Vivian was invited to holiday dinners and even vacations with the family. Not having any real family of her own in Seattle, where she met Nikki, this experience was incredibly special. At the beginning of her career, she would often create photo-shoot ideas, and Nikki was always up for modeling for her to help her implement her ideas.

Nikki has supported her in both her professional and personal growth. There was even a period of Vivian's life following her father's passing where her grief was so heartrending that she closed herself off to many friendships — including her friendship with Nikki. Fortunately, they were able to reconnect after Vivian began healing from her loss. Nikki was quick to show grace, compassion, and forgiveness towards Vivian — who admits she was not the best version of herself during her time of grief. Nikki has taught Vivian that forgiveness is a crucial part of living a deeply fulfilling life.

The next friend that Vivian listed is Mikie. Her face lit up as she explained how incredibly social he is. It is impossible for

Vivian to go anywhere in Seattle with him without them running into someone he knows. And he is not simply social, but he also raises the energy of a room with his outgoing positive nature. As a self-described introvert, Vivian admires how Mikie seems so instantly comfortable with everyone he meets. Vivian admits that due to her quiet nature, she has been misunderstood as aloof and unfriendly because she is the opposite of Mikie, preferring to move quietly around a room, and avoiding the limelight. Since Mikie's energy is contagious, simply being around him challenges Vivian to live more gregariously.

Anna, the third friend Vivian mentioned, can be described as a true boss babe. She has worked her way up through the male-dominated field of law enforcement to become a federal agent. She exudes confidence, with a zest for life. Vivian loves Anna's self-assuredness, as well as her enjoyment of travel — something they both share. Vivian is impressed by the way Anna can have a lightness about her despite the high pressures of her career. Anna's vitality makes her fun to be around, so it's easy for Vivian to vibe off her energy.

Mike is the friend Vivian described as the most generous person she knows. He has a fierce work ethic, so he works hard; yet — she doesn't know how, given his busy work schedule and dedication to his family — he also manages to find time for his friends. He has a huge heart and takes the time to be that listening ear when Vivian needs to bounce off ideas. He provides an honest male perspective on things, which more than once has allowed Vivian to see a situation differently.

Finally, while it isn't accurate to say that she saved the best for last — since all five friends bring something unique and amazing into her life — the last person she spoke of is incredibly special: her love, Garrett. Vivian and Garret were friends for ten years before they began dating. The first word that came to her to describe him was *kind*. She was quick to give his parents credit, describing them as very *kindhearted*. Vivian knows that Garrett is someone who loves her just as she is. While Vivian shared how thoughtful Garrett is and gave me examples of his day-to-day gestures of love and kindness, my heart was filled with extraordinary warmth. It helped me to remember how important it is to have a partner in life who accepts you and loves you just as you are. When I think of who I want for my children's life partners — if I could choose — it really would be someone who loves them just as they are.

At the end of our conversation, I shared with Vivian that what she admires in all her friends is what I see in her: the loyal friend; the person with great energy; the giving heart; the adventurer; and the kind, loving, and accepting life partner.

Good friends reflect our soul.

# Journal

*Today's date is:*

------------------------------------------------------------

*Journal prompt: List the five people you spend the most time with. How have they affected your behaviors, thoughts, and life?*

------------------------------------------------------------

------------------------------------------------------------

------------------------------------------------------------

------------------------------------------------------------

------------------------------------------------------------

------------------------------------------------------------

------------------------------------------------------------

------------------------------------------------------------

------------------------------------------------------------

------------------------------------------------------------

------------------------------------------------------------

------------------------------------------------------------

------------------------------------------------------------

------------------------------------------------------------

Being nice is as contagious

as a smile.

# Day 26

## What life event has led you to believe that most people are good?

Nancy
Born: Bellevue, Washington
Headstone: What you do today affects all your tomorrows

Anyone who knows Nancy would describe her as having a big heart. She is kind to everyone she meets — so it is no surprise that she also believes, without hesitation, that most people are good. I met Nancy when her eldest son and my son were in kindergarten together at a small school in Seattle. Nancy's caring nature and friendliness made me feel like we were friends from the first day I met her. We were parents at the school for only two years together, but our friendship has continued. Now both our sons are thriving in college.

*Day 26: What life event has led you to believe that most people are good?*

Nancy began our conversation by sharing with me that she loses everything. She explained that due to her ADD, losing and misplacing things is simply a way of life for her. She then proceeded to share two heart-warming stories that showed proof positive that most people are good.

One day, Nancy had taken a shopping trip to Costco. She is the mother of two athletic, active, and social boys. She has always been very involved in their schools and extra-curricular activities, so I imagine Costco has been a staple store for her family for many years. After shopping on this day, she loaded her SUV and left the parking lot for home. Unbeknownst to her, she'd left her wallet on the bumper of her SUV. By some miracle the wallet stayed on the bumper for several miles, including a brief trip down the 405 highway. It was not until she exited the highway and proceeded to turn through one of the largest multi-lane intersections in the area that her wallet flew off her bumper, landing in the middle of the street.

Not yet realizing that she had lost her wallet, she soon received a call from Alaska Airlines, her former employer. She was advised that her wallet had been found, including her Alaska Airlines ID card, and the contact information of the man who found her wallet was given to her. She met up with the man, a plumber who was traveling from one job site to the next, who handed her the wallet with everything inside. He had taken the time to retrieve the wallet from the busy intersection and to conduct some detective work to find her. Then he took time out of his busy workday to meet with her, to ensure that her wallet was returned safe and sound.

Another example solidifies Nancy's belief that most people are good. This occurred during a trip to New York City with her husband. On this evening, they were planning a beautiful dinner out, and they had tickets waiting for them to attend *The Late Show*.

Unfortunately, on a cab ride earlier that day, Nancy had left her purse inside their cab, which contained not just her wallet, but both their cell phones. While it did not take long for her to realize that she'd left her purse inside the cab, by that point the taxi had driven off and quickly became indistinguishable amidst the sea of yellow cabs that filled the streets. Instead of their planned night out, they spent their evening cancelling credit cards, and they no longer had the contact number for the show's tickets. So, they missed the show, and spent the evening at the hotel.

They flew home the next morning. Weeks later, a package arrived in the mail. The writing on the package appeared to be from someone for whom English may not have been a first language. The package contained Nancy's purse with its entire contents, including the cash she had left in the purse. Nancy was so grateful that she sent a reward back to the return address.

While talking to Nancy about these amazing experiences, she shared a fun story with me. She is always the customer at the register when the tape runs out and the cashier must apologize for the interruption and change the tape — or she inevitably gets the receipt with the pink line running down the center. It happens to Nancy so often that it has become a running joke with her friends and family. At one point, it was happening so frequently that she had the fleeting thought that maybe it was a bad omen.

While attending a convention with her husband, one of the hired entertainers was a fortune teller. Nancy described her constant experience with the register tapes, and the fortune teller told her that the reason it happened so much was to allow people to be in her presence longer.

After being given that positive explanation, Nancy not only thinks it is funny that she is the customer who always must wait for the register tape to be changed but now she welcomes the extra gift of time with the cashier. I think the fortune teller's explanation makes a lot of sense because it *is* a gift to spend time with someone like Nancy — a person who not only has a heart of gold but who also firmly believes that most people are inherently good.

# Journal

*Today's date is:*

_____

*Journal prompt: What life event has led you to believe that most people are good?*

_____
_____
_____
_____
_____
_____
_____
_____
_____
_____
_____
_____
_____
_____
_____

# *Day 27*

## What is a disagreement you had that helped shape the person you are today?

Sheila
Born: Santa Clara, California
Headstone: Don't start the party without me

Sheila and I have known one another for years, but this was the first time that we carved out time to share a meal together, to really sit down and have a full conversation rather than the very limited bursts of dialogue that we've experienced at large gatherings in the past. It was a gorgeous warm day in June, and we met on a restaurant deck overlooking Lake Washington at a popular spot located just east of Seattle. Other than the few mighty gusts of wind — which made us pause a couple of times to ensure our menus didn't fly away — it was the perfect June afternoon.

*Day 27: What is a disagreement you had that helped shape the person you are today?*

The disagreement that Shelia described to me carries such heavy significance that it was the catalyst that ended her fourteen-year marriage.

Sheila came from a large family. She is the youngest of six children. She was raised in Cupertino, California — a city not only known to be Apple's headquarters; but also ranked as number twenty-seven in *Money*'s "Best Places to Live" (2012); and also regularly listed as one of "America's Best Small Towns." Furthermore, in 2014, Movoto Real Estate ranked Cupertino the seventh "Happiest Suburb" in the United States — ranking highly in the categories of income, safety, marriage, and education. Sheila had what sounds to me like an ideal all-American family upbringing.

Being the youngest child, she witnessed her older siblings marry and have kids. She presumed — like everyone around her, without question — that she would follow in her siblings' traditional path. However, Sheila never felt a particular urgency to have children, even though she was open to the possibility. She simply figured that she would know when she was ready to start a family because when the time was right, she would feel a natural desire to become a mother.

Sheila got married at twenty-nine years of age, to a man who went to the same college she attended. They began dating not too long after college, after running into each other at a social gathering with mutual friends. The church where they were married strongly recommended that they participate in an Engaged Encounter weekend — which is a part of the Marriage Encounter program.

My husband and I had also attended one of these weekends before we got married — probably around the same time Sheila and her fiancé did — so I was familiar with the weekend that she described. This is a weekend in which both people are provided with journals; they listen to presentations; and they are asked to individually write letters or journal entries around suggested topics. The journals' writings are exchanged with one another throughout the weekend. (This is a communication style that is encouraged to continue throughout the marriage. While I know many young couples who attended one of these types of engagement weekends through their respective churches, I'm sorry to say I do not know even one couple who has maintained the journal-writing style of communication.)

Sheila told me that one of the writing prompts was about starting a family. Looking back at what they had each written in their journals, they appeared to be on the same page: Both were neither hot nor cold to the idea of kids. Both looked at having kids as a possibility they would visit together in the future.

Not long after their wedding day, questions about starting a family quickly arose — not just from friends and family but also from new acquaintances. The question was never *Are you going to have kids?* Instead, the question was always *When are you going to have kids?* Often, the conversations felt very awkward. Sheila did her best to steer away from what she viewed as a very personal matter. As she processed the question of kids, she became more aware that perhaps children weren't a part of her future. Initially, when she shared with family members that she wasn't sure if she ever wanted kids, their responses felt dismissive.

At the time that Sheila was going through this period of self-realization, she was in her 30s, and it seemed that everyone around her was having kids. She didn't have a group of peers who had chosen not to have children. She now knows several women who made the same decision she did. If only she had known these women during her 30s, she wouldn't have felt so alone in her decision.

The questions about having children grew in prominence during her marriage. It moved from just a passing conversation to becoming a sticking point. She began to feel considerable pressure from her husband to start a family. Soon she noticed that the subject was coming up more and more often — centered around his desire to have kids without taking into consideration her feelings. During all the pressure and soul searching, she in fact discovered that she was physically unable to have a child. Sheila is part of a small percentage of women who experience menopause while still in their 30s. Subsequently, by that point, she thought having kids was off the table.

For a couple of years, the subject was quiet. Then, her husband started his own crusade to finding ways to have kids. He even suggested hiring a surrogate — focusing again on his needs and not taking into consideration Shelia's desires. While she respects other couples who embrace various options for creating a family, she knew that having kids was simply not meant for her.

Being pressured to have a child by alternative means was not only stressful, but it also resulted in the end of her marriage. Sheila had to stand up for herself. While in some ways it may have been easier for her to go along with her husband's desire to have kids and follow society's expectations of her as a married woman in her 30s, she recognized that doing so would have been a selfish act — and not the way a child should be brought into the world.

It took time for Sheila to become comfortable with her decision not to have children. It took time for her not to feel brought down by the judgment of others. She eventually learned how to let people know that she didn't want kids without feeling like she had to explain further. She didn't need to make the other person feel better or to justify her feelings — something she had frequently done when she was younger.

Sheila's experience has given her empathy for individuals who find that they must expose parts of their lives to strangers — constantly having to explain their identity or their life choices.

The journey to end her marriage was not easy. Through the process, grappling with the most significant life-shaping disagreement she ever experienced, Sheila learned that a woman's value comes from many facets. And it is for her alone to define — not for anyone else.

# Journal

*Today's date is:*

------------------------------------------------------------

*Journal prompt:* What is a disagreement you had that helped shape the person you are today?

------------------------------------------------------------

------------------------------------------------------------

------------------------------------------------------------

------------------------------------------------------------

------------------------------------------------------------

------------------------------------------------------------

------------------------------------------------------------

------------------------------------------------------------

------------------------------------------------------------

------------------------------------------------------------

------------------------------------------------------------

------------------------------------------------------------

------------------------------------------------------------

------------------------------------------------------------

"Don't waste a mess by ignoring
the message."
— Shari Leid

# *Day 28*

# What have you learned about love?

Stephanie

Born: Seattle

Headstone: She was fun, a friend, and kind to everyone she met

Stephanie and I have known each other for years, primarily seeing one another at large parties. Thankfully, in the past three years, we've made it a point to get together outside of the large gatherings to share a meal or coffee — to simply talk one-on-one — which has nurtured our friendship. I love being in group photos with Stephanie — because while a lot of our girlfriends are tall, Stephanie is petite like me, so she helps balance out group shots that I am in. It makes me smile when I see that I'm not the only one standing a head shorter than the rest in the photo capture!

*Day 28: What have you learned about love?*

Stephanie told me that when she thinks about love, she thinks about the two men who came into her life at different times: first, her ex-husband to whom she was married for over twenty years; and second, her current long-term love, a man she has enjoyed life with for the past six-plus years. Because I met Stephanie after her divorce, I've never met her ex-husband. It was fun to hear the story of how they met as young college students and of the life they created together.

When Stephanie talks about her ex-husband, she speaks with kindness, and even a bit of laughter. They met at the University of Oregon, where he was a transfer student from the East coast; she was an undergrad there for all four years. She believes they both went on their first date essentially just to get their Jewish mothers off their backs. At the time they attended, the Jewish student population was incredibly small. Stephanie recalls that there were only about 200 Jewish students out of the entire population of undergraduate students at this huge university. Despite not knowing one another personally, both mothers were over the moon when they learned there was a possibility that their kids would go out on a date.

To both their moms' delight, that first date turned into a courtship that lasted over five years, followed by a wedding, and two sons. While their marriage wasn't solely based on timing or a checklist, there definitely was some of that involved. Go to college, get married, have kids: check, check, check. The young couple purchased a home and enjoyed a relatively ideal and comfortable suburban lifestyle.

While she didn't discuss with me the impetus for the divorce, we did move our conversation back to the question at hand: *What have you learned about love?* This is when Stephanie's face lit up as she spoke about her current partner, a man with whom she has fallen madly in love. And through the relationship, she has learned that love is kind. Before meeting her current love, she never really thought about how much kindness is a part of love. That is what she has learned from this relationship.

She describes the man she is with as caring and thoughtful, which makes her feel constantly loved without question. This makes it easy for her to love him back with the same affection and warmth. It's not grand gestures that are important, but simply the everyday sweetness he shows by the way he interacts with her — the small considerate things he does each day.

Our conversation made me think about my own relationship. There was a time when my husband and I were struggling. We seemed to be angry often. One day I woke up and decided to treat our relationship with grace and gratitude — and that decision changed everything. It changed the way I communicated, and it allowed me to see all the good that luckily outweighed the bad in our relationship. I also started to notice his many acts of kindness, which he did each day. And, whenever I proceeded with grace and gratitude, he responded likewise — with gentleness and kindliness. Stephanie's words truly hit home for me!

# Journal

*Today's date is:*

-------------------------------------------------------------

*Journal prompt: What have you learned about love?*

-------------------------------------------------------------

-------------------------------------------------------------

-------------------------------------------------------------

-------------------------------------------------------------

-------------------------------------------------------------

-------------------------------------------------------------

-------------------------------------------------------------

-------------------------------------------------------------

-------------------------------------------------------------

-------------------------------------------------------------

-------------------------------------------------------------

-------------------------------------------------------------

-------------------------------------------------------------

-------------------------------------------------------------

-------------------------------------------------------------

-------------------------------------------------------------

-------------------------------------------------------------

"Love is fluid — it ebbs and flows —
and is magical."
— Shari Leid

# Day 29

## Who is the most optimistic person you know?

Trina
Born: Seattle
Headstone: Blessed kind soul with a joyous heart

Trina and I met through one of Trina's life-long best friends, Dana Frank, who authored the Foreword in *Make Your Mess Your Message* (the second book in the *Friendship* series). I'm not surprised that Trina and Dana have been best friends since middle school. They are both outgoing, possessing an energy that naturally attracts others to them. Trina is gorgeous, with a beautiful smile. While happily in her fifth decade, she could easily be mistaken for a woman in her 30s.

*Day 29: Who is the most optimistic person you know?*

At the time we met for dinner, Trina was still very much a newlywed, married for just shy of a year. Although not married for very long, she and her husband have been together for nearly seven years. It is easy to see why their relationship works. He, like

Trina, is easy to talk to from the moment you meet him. And I'm guessing he can talk to just about anyone, about anything. He's the type of dinner guest you know you could seat anywhere at the table, and whoever would be seated next to him would have a great night of lively fun and easy conversation.

When Trina shared with me that the most optimistic person she knows is her husband, I immediately thought how fortunate she is to have found a life partner who walks through life with a glass-half-full perspective. I was curious to learn if optimism came naturally to him or if it's something that he has worked to cultivate.

Trina explained that her husband has practiced Buddhism for much of his life, including a whole year of living in Japan at a monastery with Buddhist monks. His practice grounds him to live life with compassion and purpose. Recognizing that suffering, just as joy, is a part of life, he embraces life in its entirety.

Trina described her husband's philosophy, something they have in common, for which she is grateful: Every time life has knocked her down, even during some difficult experiences, she knows that there is a teaching moment — that the setback is leading her in a new direction. Her comments remind me of one of my favorite books by Ryan Holiday, *The Obstacle Is the Way*. Seeing obstacles as detours rather than roadblocks not only helps us to notice how many options are always available; it also allows us room for unexpected opportunities to come to fruition.

Optimism is contagious. Trina witnesses the fact that while living with her husband's optimism influences her, it also has a positive effect on her teenage son. Because Trina's husband was raised by a mother who also practices Buddhism, being optimistic seems almost innate to him. But even if you didn't grow up with optimism, it is a mental state that can be consciously learned and practiced by anyone.

Towards the end of our dinner, Trina shared one of her husband's favorite quotes, from motivational speaker Les Brown: "When life knocks you down, try to land on your back. Because if you can look up, you can get up. Let your reason get you back up."

# Journal

*Today's date is:*

_____

*Journal prompt: Who is the most optimistic person you know?*

_____
_____
_____
_____
_____
_____
_____
_____
_____
_____
_____
_____
_____
_____
_____

"Optimism, like a smile, is contagious."
— Shari Leid

# Day 30

## Who deserves credit in your life whom you are slow to acknowledge?

Rebecca
Born: Seattle
Headstone: She lived for her family, to laugh, and have fun.
Always looking toward light, she followed the sun. Never ready
to leave, but still a hell of a run.

I love to hear people tell stories of how they met. We just never know how meeting one person can lead to an entirely new web of connections and experiences. Rebecca and I met through a chance connection with a now-mutual friend. She met our mutual girlfriend, Lydia, at a public park. They struck up a conversation while their kids played, and it led to a wonderful friendship. Lydia and I met just a few years prior to Rebecca's chance meeting with her — when we spotted one another across the room at a fundraising event. Lydia and I were much younger than most of the event's attendees, so we were naturally drawn to one another. Rebecca and I then met when we were both invited to Lydia's daughter's birthday party. And that was nearly ten years ago — our "how we met" story.

Day 30: *Who deserves credit in your life whom you are slow to acknowledge?*

Speaking of "how we met" stories, Rebecca met her husband twenty years ago at what was one of Seattle's most iconic bars, J&M Café, established in 1889 and located in Seattle's iconic Pioneer Square. It had been a fixture for Seattle's bar-hopping young singles and old-timers for generations. Their meeting must have been in the stars that night, because Scott just happened to be in town on a short visit from his home state of California. Now, having celebrated their sixteenth wedding anniversary earlier this year, they are parents of three beautiful children, and they work together as fitness and healthy-eating coaches. They've created a literally picture-perfect life together. I've told Rebecca more than once that she has the most photogenic family. Her family photos always catch my eye as I scroll through my social media feed.

During our meeting, Rebecca took a moment to text her husband to confirm their son's pick-up from a sports practice. Partnering up as parents, business partners, and as husband and wife, they clearly are an effective team. It may be a surprise to some that despite their close relationship, it is her husband whom she has been slow to acknowledge. Rebecca says he deserves a lot of credit in her life.

I've met Rebecca's husband on a couple of occasions, but I haven't had the opportunity to really get to know him. After listening to Rebecca share what an exceptional person he is, there is no doubt that those who have the good fortune to be friends with Scott are folks who have someone who will show up for them when needed. Scott is always the guy in their corner.

Rebecca shared that he has always wanted her to succeed and shine, recognizing her artistic talents and culinary skills. Even from early in their dating years, when she was making healthy smoothies for friends, he encouraged her to capitalize on her culinary gift, to meet the community's need for healthy smoothies. He suggested that she build a website to market the juices. And in most recent years, while already having an established fitness business, he encouraged her to come on as a partner. He recognized her natural skill and keen interest in nutrition and healthy living. He knew she could help him support clients in their pursuit of eating clean and healthy as they work on gaining physical strength, increased flexibility, cardio health, and fat loss through their individually designed training programs. Scott and Rebecca now have an established full-service fitness company, Fast Eat Live (www.fasteatlive.com).

Scott's desire to support and cheer on Rebecca is the way he carries himself with everyone he meets. He is passionate about wanting all people to be the best version of themselves. It pains him when he sees someone failing to thrive.

Rebecca shared a tender story that captures Scott's caring spirit. She recalls being in the car with him when they were stopped at a red light, looking over, and noticing a change in his expression. He looked sad, and really bothered. She wasn't sure what happened to cause his change in expression. When she asked, Scott explained that he was thinking about the homeless person they had seen on the side of the road, and he wished that he could do something to improve that person's life. When Scott looks at someone, he sees the good — the potential for greatness.

While Rebecca credits Scott for making her a better person, and for being her biggest support and life cheerleader, she admits that she hasn't told him as much and isn't sure why. She finds it easy to share with friends what they mean to her, but for some reason it is hard for her to tell her own husband. I imagine that it is common for spouses to neglect sharing with one another how much they mean to each other and how much they've helped each other thrive — especially spouses who met in their 20s and have grown up together.

I admit I am guilty of this, too. My husband and I have been together for twenty-seven years, married for twenty-five, and I have never taken the time to share with him the incredibly positive impact that I know he has made in my life. Just having this conversation with Rebecca has made me keenly aware of how big that impact has been.

We laughed at how surprised her husband will be when he reads this chapter. I imagine this chapter will be a gift for him, and for their marriage. I trust it will be the catalyst for a conversation filled with recognition and gratitude for the important impact he has made on Rebecca's life.

# Journal

*Today's date is:*

------------------------------------------------

*Journal prompt:* Who deserves credit in your life whom you are slow to acknowledge?

------------------------------------------------

------------------------------------------------

------------------------------------------------

------------------------------------------------

------------------------------------------------

------------------------------------------------

------------------------------------------------

------------------------------------------------

------------------------------------------------

------------------------------------------------

------------------------------------------------

------------------------------------------------

------------------------------------------------

------------------------------------------------

------------------------------------------------

------------------------------------------------

# Day 31

## What is the secret to a good marriage?

Heidi
Born: Seattle
Headstone: Be Relentless

When Heidi and I met, my children were in their early years of grade school and Heidi had just given birth to her second child. She signed up for a fitness class that I was teaching, and we instantly hit it off. Heidi is a gifted photographer (www.heidileonardphotography.com), specializing in child and family portraits. She has taken many of my favorite family annual photos throughout the years. Whenever I meet someone in my area of town who is looking for a photographer who will provide museum-quality portraits, I always recommend Heidi — not only because she is a friend, but because I believe she is incredibly talented, with a keen artistic eye.

*Day 31: What is the secret to a good marriage?*

While I've known Heidi for many years, I've yet to meet her husband of fifteen years. Heidi describes herself as an extrovert and her husband as an introvert. He prefers smaller gatherings, and he will almost always choose an evening at home rather than a large social gathering. He is content spending time at home with his family, watching a good movie, or simply reading a great book.

When I mentioned to Heidi that she and her husband seem to have very different personalities, she quickly and enthusiastically agreed, exclaiming, "Yes, we're very different!"

I find her enthusiasm around their differences refreshing. More commonly, I hear my girlfriends describe devastating relationship break-ups with the sentiment, "We were too different."

So how does Heidi embrace their differences? How does she manage to have a marriage that not only survives the differences but continues to grow and thrive?

Heidi and her husband met eighteen years ago. Heidi was a member of a rowing club located off the shores of Lake Union in Seattle. The group rowed early each Saturday morning, followed by a much-loved weekly brunch together. She was an established member of the club at the time her husband happened to walk in, interested in joining the rowing club. Upon seeing him, Heidi immediately thought, *Who's the cute new guy?*

Not shy, Heidi was known as the icebreaker of the group. She would sit across from a new member during brunch and learn all about that person, utilizing her gift for conversation and her genuine interest in others. True to form on that fateful morning, she sat across from the man who would later become her husband, learning all she could about him. When he said he was from the East coast, she naturally asked what brought him to Washington state. When he shared that a girlfriend was the catalyst for his cross-country move, she assumed he was still with that girlfriend, so she didn't dive further into his relationship status. He continued to show up for Saturday rowing sessions and brunch — so it was not long before she found out that he was single, having ended the former relationship over a year before he'd joined the club.

Heidi and her husband dated for a year before becoming engaged, and they were engaged for a year before marrying. Now in their sixteenth year of marriage, their lives are busy with three children, an elderly dog, and two thriving careers. Heidi is an accomplished family photographer, with the gift of capturing the personalities of children in a unique way unparalleled by other photographers in her field.

Becoming parents was something both Heidi and her husband discussed prior to marriage. Her husband was raised Irish Catholic. At the time she met him, he was no longer practicing Catholicism and in general he was not in favor of organized religion. Heidi, on the other hand, was raised in the Jewish faith. Heidi made it clear to her husband that it was important to her that their children be raised Jewish. Despite her husband's distaste for organized religion, he recognized how important Heidi's faith is to her — and because it meant so much to her — he fully supports her in that regard, allowing her to take the lead on all matters relating to their children's religious upbringing in Judaism.

Heidi laughed as she shared that for her daughter's bat mitzvah, without complaint, her husband not only put on a nice suit, but he also sat in the front row at the service with a twinkle in his eye, very obviously proud of their daughter as she presented her Torah portion at the temple. For a couple who has such profoundly different religious beliefs, the fact that they are able to come to an agreement on how religious faith will be handled in raising their children is an accomplishment to be admired.

Religion is not the only compromise Heidi and her husband have navigated in their marriage. It was impossible to ignore their fundamental social differences. As mentioned earlier, Heidi's husband is content with staying at home. Meanwhile, socializing fuels Heidi's soul. Because of this difference in their personality types, Heidi will happily attend events by herself, or with her girlfriends, rather than with her husband. That said, when her husband realizes that an event is important to her — one that she would really like him to attend, such as their children's school auctions, which Heidi puts a lot of volunteer time into — he shows up without complaint to support her. He knows when to show up and when it is okay for him to sit on the sidelines. Heidi knows when to ask him to join her and when she'll have more fun going out with her friends.

As we spoke, it became apparent to me that the secret to a good marriage is not about agreeing on everything or having the same personality type. The secret to a good marriage is about respecting each other's differences; allowing one another to grow; and trusting that if asked, the other person will be there, no matter what.

# Journal

*Today's date is:*

----------------------------------------

*Journal prompt: What is the secret to a good marriage?*

----------------------------------------

----------------------------------------

----------------------------------------

----------------------------------------

----------------------------------------

----------------------------------------

----------------------------------------

----------------------------------------

----------------------------------------

----------------------------------------

----------------------------------------

----------------------------------------

----------------------------------------

----------------------------------------

# Day 32

# What relationships are adding to your life?

Lyanne
Born: Seattle
Headstone: Loved God and Loved Others

Lyanne and I are lifelong friends. We met as toddlers in the nursery classroom at our parents' church — a church where she is still a very active member. In fact, her husband has been the Associate Pastor there for years. I knew I wanted to speak with Lyanne as part of my *Friendship* series, but I kept putting off asking her. Knowing Lyanne as I do, I was pretty sure that our conversation — whatever the question — would lead to a discussion about her faith and the church we grew up in, because both are a central part of her life. I was hesitant to set the date simply because we both know that my experience and beliefs differ from hers. While I know our friendship is heart-centered, and any discussion we have is respectful, this issue still has the potential to create a painful moment for each of us.

Day 32: *What relationships are adding to your life?*

As Lyanne points out, this question leaves room for interpretation. So, I told her to answer it simply the way she reads it. She explained that the relationships she has in her life all add something. They are very strong — many dating back to childhood and the church we grew up in.

Lyanne, like me, is adopted, and she has the most remarkable parents. When Lyanne explains how supportive her mom and dad have always been — and that she always felt like she was a part of the family, with adoption never being an issue — I believe her. Thinking back to our childhood, I recall that her mother was the one who frequently planned fun arts-and-crafts projects for our playdates, and I remember her making us sandwiches (*Fun fact*: Lyanne's mom is the person who taught me that peanut butter goes on the bread before the jelly, or you can't spread it — a life-long lesson that has served me well). Her father, who was an educator — a teacher who later became a vice principal — was adored by his students. Whenever I meet people my age and I learn that that they were a student at a school where Lyanne's dad worked, I immediately ask if they remember her dad. Without fail, their faces light up and they tell me what a wonderful teacher he was.

Lyanne's parents were much closer to many of the other church members than my parents were — traveling together and sharing meals together throughout the week. As a child I spent a lot of time at Lyanne's home. It was commonplace for a church member to stop by and enjoy time at her house, whether it was for a meal or simply to watch TV and hang out. The community that her parents created this way among family and friends fostered Lyanne's sense of belonging.

Lyanne explained that the community her parents formed included families with children of all ages — many who were older than she and her younger sister were, because her parents were older when they began their family. Looking back, she appreciates the memories of kids who were older than she was who took time to hang out with her and take her to fun places like an arcade or a movie theatre. She had a network of older kids who were always willing to take time out of their busy teenage and young-adult lives to cheer her on at her basketball games — a constant means of support. It is hard for her to imagine what her life would have been like if she didn't have such nurturing friendships — especially with the older kids who seemed to always be there to support her and her sister.

Lyanne's friendships are not limited to her church family but also extend to additional childhood, high school, and college friends, as well as work colleagues who have become life-long friends. Lyanne has been a grade-school teacher since the early 1990s. She still gets together with the group of teacher friends she began teaching with nearly thirty years ago.

I've always said — somewhat jokingly but also quite seriously — that most friendships run their course in seven years, because friendships naturally ebb and flow. It is okay that friendships end. Lyanne has very few friendships that have ended. Sure, some have faded because of distance and time, but her large core group of friends has remained the same. She has maintained loyal friends throughout the years, now raising children alongside one another.

Lyanne and her husband are raising their daughter the way Lyanne was raised — surrounded by close friends and family. Most of them attend their church — and again it's children of all ages engaging and caring for one another.

My biggest takeaway from speaking with Lyanne is that we as adults can create community for our children — and for the young people we mentor. Creating community goes beyond the occasional neighborhood playgroup for our kids. Cultivating family relationships is important, as it allows children to witness adults interacting with each other. Lyanne's life experience is an example of how our relationships as adults can positively affect our children.

Speaking to Lyanne turned out to be not as uncomfortable as I'd initially feared. Our conversation left me wondering how two children growing up in what outwardly seems like the same environment can have very different experiences. I cannot pinpoint one thing that made our experience of being raised in the same church so different. Perhaps the answer can be found somewhere in a complex nature-vs.-nurture debate.

Lyanne's keen ability to maintain relationships is evident in our own friendship. Despite our substantially different religious beliefs, we are still able to share ideas. I know that if anything ever happened to one of us where one of us needed the other, we would each absolutely show up for the other.

And that is what this *Friendship* series is all about. This project is about learning from one another, finding a connection, and recognizing that despite our differences we can find a common voice, and common life experiences, which lead us to discovering common ground — with every person we meet.

Everyone you meet is both your teacher and your student. We are here to learn, grow, and live together with compassion, love, and understanding.

# Journal

*Today's date is:*

-------------------------------------------------

*Journal prompt: What relationships are adding to your life?*

-------------------------------------------------

-------------------------------------------------

-------------------------------------------------

-------------------------------------------------

-------------------------------------------------

-------------------------------------------------

-------------------------------------------------

-------------------------------------------------

-------------------------------------------------

-------------------------------------------------

-------------------------------------------------

-------------------------------------------------

-------------------------------------------------

-------------------------------------------------

-------------------------------------------------

# Ask Yourself This

# Adulting:
# Shari's Own Reflections

1. *List the five people you spend the most time with. How have they affected your behaviors, thoughts, and life?* 1) My husband, whom I have been with since I was twenty-five years old, has been the most influential person in my life. He has taught me what it means to love and support another person. I can't imagine what my life would have looked like if I had not met and married him. He has always supported me without feeling the need to control or compete. He has been the best life partner. 2) My daughter, through her struggles with school due to her learning differences, has taught me how to celebrate and understand myself and others. I've learned from her that we all have our own journey, and my children's journeys aren't mine to own or control. 3) My son has taught me what it is like to be a guy, and how simple and complex guys truly are. Because I am adopted, and he is my biological child, he is the only person I have in my life whom I'm biologically related to. I see much of myself through him.

And, 4) and 5) I was recently asked by a girlfriend, "Who are your best friends?" It was a fair question, but I didn't have a simple answer. I spend an equal amount of time with all my friends, so I do not have two people who stand out as my "go-to two." Sometimes I wonder if I should try to cultivate a best friend or a best-friend group. Nevertheless, my purpose in this lifetime is to meet, connect, support, and guide others. For this reason, I've been blessed with many friends who come in and out of my life. Most of the friends who have been in and out of my life over the past three years have been memorialized in my *Friendship* series.

2. *What life event has led you to believe that most people are good?* I believe it's true: Most people are good. When I was twenty-two years old, I was involved in a serious head-on collision. A woman who lived not far from the accident scene ran to my vehicle, and while I floated in and out of consciousness while still trapped inside my car, she managed to obtain all my identifying information while waiting for the medics to arrive. She received my parents' phone number from me and was able to call them after she returned to her home (This was long before cell phones).

My condition was dire, and the jaws of life were required to cut me out of my vehicle. I was rushed to Harborview Hospital, the region's only level-one trauma hospital. The woman who stayed with me until medical help arrived did not know me from Adam and she never saw me again — but she was with me at one of the most frightening times of my life. That experience showed me how much love and comfort can come from a stranger — an outstanding example of how most people are good.

3. *What is a disagreement you had that helped shape the person you are today?* I had a disagreement surrounding racism with a woman who is in the first book of the *Friendship* series. Part of the craziness about this is that we are on the same side; yet we communicate, process, argue, and express our opinions in very different ways. She was a close friend, and I will always love her; I would still do anything for her if called upon. The disagreement was incredibly painful. This experience changed the way I share my opinions on sensitive matters such as race relations and politics. In many ways it quieted my voice and left me hesitant to speak publicly on sensitive matters. Ultimately, I know I will find my public voice on these subjects again. And when I do, I will have been shaped into a more thoughtful speaker because of this painful disagreement.

4. *What have you learned about love?* Just as with a smile, you get what you give.

5. *Who is the most optimistic person you know?* My husband, Rory. He isn't the type who walks around all Pollyanna, always thinking the glass is half full; but when things don't go his way, he doesn't dwell on them. He acknowledges when things go sideways but then keeps moving forward. I think that his ability to handle life in this way is what makes him the successful trial attorney he is.

6. *Who deserves credit in your life whom you are slow to acknowledge?* I'm repeating myself, but it's true: The answer again is my husband, Rory. I hope that I'm making up for it here! We started dating when we were only twenty-five years old, and we have been together for over half our lives. It is easy to take someone for granted when you've been together for that long — but I really must credit him for growing alongside me and supporting all of my projects and ambitions. I couldn't imagine a better life partner. Maybe he'll tear up when reading this. He tends to be more emotional than I am. He would probably disagree and let you know he is a rock — and then he would laugh. I guess it is probably more accurate to say that he is more of a sentimentalist than I am.

7. *What is the secret to a good marriage?* Since our twentieth wedding anniversary, each year we have a meeting on our anniversary to decide whether we wish to stay together for the next year. This is not my husband's favorite conversation; but I love it, because when we decide that we are going to stay together, we are acknowledging that we are in this relationship and marriage by choice. Neither one of us is stuck. We want to be here! I think in a long marriage, it is easy to get to the point where you feel trapped, and then you fall into victim mode, which is not good for any relationship. Remembering that you are in your marriage by choice is my secret to a good marriage.

8. *What relationships are adding to your life?* All my girlfriends in the *Friendship* series. I continue to learn from all of them, and I'm grateful to have the pleasure of walking through this journey of life with them. As I said repeatedly in the first book of the *Friendship* series, I believe that everyone I meet is both my teacher and my student.

# Ask Yourself This

## Today

I love to get a good
night's rest — often it solves
everything.

# Day 33

## When you're down, what makes you feel better?

Michelle
Born: Los Angeles, California
Headstone: She lived a life with no regrets

When I think of Michelle, the word *warmth* immediately pops into my head. Michelle has a natural gentleness and sweetness to her that instantly makes you feel cared for. She freely offers her home as a gathering place for friends. In fact, I met Michelle when we were new to the same area of town, and she used a Facebook neighborhood group to invite women to socialize over a weekly night of wine, snacks, and a little reality TV–viewing at her home. She is someone who does not hesitate to help a person in need, even a new acquaintance. So, while she naturally makes people feel watched over, I wondered what makes *her* feel nurtured. More specifically, I wanted to know: What makes Michelle feel better when she is down?

*Day 33: When you're down, what makes you feel better?*

Michelle initially joked that her answer to the question I posed is, "Champagne!" She told me that until I asked the question, she never gave a thought to what she does for comfort when she is feeling down. To her surprise and mine, she realized that her answer is prayer.

She talks to God when she needs comfort. This is interesting to me, since she did not grow up attending church, and she doesn't attend church now. She is not particularly religious. If pushed, she may say she identifies with Catholicism, but much of that is intertwined with cultural tradition more than formal religion. She didn't grow up praying. Her parents, both immigrants from Cuba, grew up in a Cuba that didn't allow the practice of religion.

Michelle describes herself as a control freak. So, when she feels she doesn't have control, when life is going sideways, she feels herself becoming agitated and upset. She finds that taking a moment in prayer — putting the situation into God's hands — allows her to let go of control and provides her with feelings of peace and calmness.

I must admit, until my conversation with Michelle, I'd always correlated prayer with religion. I didn't realize that I thought that way until speaking with her. I was raised in a family that considered themselves Born-Again Christians, for whom prayer was something very ingrained as a *duty* in my household. When I left my extremely conservative Christian upbringing, I moved away from prayer during my 20s and 30s. Now in my 50s, I acknowledge that I *do* pray and talk to God quite frequently.

Michelle's view of separating prayer from organized religion feels comforting to me. Religion can be so polarizing and is often politicized. The gift of separating prayer as a practice tied to an organized religion feels like a huge, freeing exhale — dropping the baggage that religion can carry. Our conversation reminded me that you can have a religion based in doctrine without a personal relationship with God; and you can have a personal relationship with God without religion.

At the time we spoke, Michelle was seven months pregnant with her second child. We happened to have a day of record-breaking heat in the Seattle area, hitting 109 degrees Fahrenheit. Michelle's house, like many in the area, isn't equipped with centralized air conditioning. And to add to the uncomfortable conditions she was experiencing, she and her family were just three days away from moving from Washington state to California. To top it all off, the movers she hired had just cancelled that day. I also saw her young son in the background, engrossed with an activity at a desk. Her husband, who works in IT, was called in to work, so she didn't have his help to watch their son as planned during our meeting. (Luckily this turned out not to be a problem because her son was so engrossed in his activity, he didn't mind me stealing his mom away for a bit.) And, to add one more glitch, we had to meet via FaceTime instead of our planned Zoom meeting because the internet at her home had gone down due to a power outage caused by the heat wave. Yes, for sure, Michelle was having a full day. Yet she seemed calm and composed. It's no surprise: Today, she had lain down for a moment and prayed.

# Journal

*Today's date is:*

---

*When you're down, what makes you feel better?*

---

---

---

---

---

---

---

---

---

---

---

---

---

"Coffee is my morning hug."
— Shari Leid

# Day 34

## What do you complain about more than anything else?

Nicole
Born in Orange, California
Headstone: In all things she moved forward with both her heart and her mind

Nicole and I met over a decade ago when I worked as a fitness instructor, training clients from my in-home studio. From the moment I met Nicole, I was immediately drawn to her sarcastic and often self-deprecating dry wit. She is one of those friends who makes you smile when you think of her because of her wicked sense of humor. A former college athlete, she possesses the drive and mindset that most elite athletes have. I loved leading the fitness classes that she attended because her hard work brought the energy in the room up a notch. She kept everyone, including myself, motivated to work harder.

*Day 34: What do you complain about more than anything else?*

Neither of us resides in the same neighborhood or city where we met. We now live nearly two hours away from one another, so this meeting we had, on a sunny afternoon in May, was a treat. It was the first time we had seen each other in about three years, but we found that we were able to pick up our conversation as if no time had passed — the way good friends are able to do naturally.

For Nicole, her biggest complaint comes when she sees someone stuck and not moving forward. Nicole has an athlete's mindset, which helps her to face challenges head on. She also comes from a family where problems were handled right away, as they presented themselves. Her parents always led by example. Her dad, a former U.S. Marine as well as a former collegiate wrestler, was someone who not only looked at matters with a big-picture perspective, he also continuously moved forward. Her mom and two brothers are very similar in nature. One example Nicole shared is that her younger brother, who was born with an auditory processing disorder, not only overcame his disability; he surpassed it and is now fluent in English, Spanish, Dutch, Sranantongo, and Tongan!

Obviously, Nicole has come from a family of doers. She always moves forward despite the circumstances because this is a practice that's been ingrained in her throughout her upbringing.

Similar to an athletic coach who believes in her players, Nicole believes in everyone's ability to move forward, even if it happens with baby steps. It is easy to feel stuck when you're in the middle of difficult circumstances, but here are a few steps that she hopes will help:

1. Take a step away from the emotions of the situation.

2. Know that you always have options.

3. Grab a piece of paper and brainstorm solutions. Include even options that seem far-fetched. Dream big. After completion, set the list aside.

4. Return to the list the next day. Narrow your options down to the ones that seem most desirable and/or doable.

5. Define small incremental steps you can take to move forward.

6. Write down three good things you can focus on in your current situation. Take your focus off the bad things.

7. Ask yourself, "Am I worrying about something that has not yet happened?" If you are, decide that you won't give that worry any more of your energy. Worrying does not solve anything, and the very thing you are worrying about may never happen.

8. Let go of paralysis by analyses — and commit to taking just *one* step today.

Nicole comes from a family that believes in moving forward and looking for opportunities even in the chaos. Fortunately, this ability to move forward from difficult circumstances is a skill that can be learned and practiced by anyone.

# Journal

*Today's date is:*

-------------------------------------------------------------------

*Journal prompt: What do you complain about more than anything else?*

-------------------------------------------------------------------

-------------------------------------------------------------------

-------------------------------------------------------------------

-------------------------------------------------------------------

-------------------------------------------------------------------

-------------------------------------------------------------------

-------------------------------------------------------------------

-------------------------------------------------------------------

-------------------------------------------------------------------

-------------------------------------------------------------------

-------------------------------------------------------------------

-------------------------------------------------------------------

-------------------------------------------------------------------

-------------------------------------------------------------------

"Complaining is the first step; the second step is to do something!"
— Shari Leid

# Day 35

## Was there a time in your life when you needed extreme courage to keep going because others gave up?

Kathryn
Born: Seattle
Headstone: Life is a dance

I met Kathryn through a wonderful group of girlfriends. When I met her, I connected effortlessly. We learned that we are both mothers of beautiful daughters who we adopted from China — and we both adopted from the same agency, Holt International, which also happens to be the agency that facilitated my own adoption in 1970. Having this unique connection with Kathryn makes her automatically feel like family to me.

*Day 35: Was there a time in your life when you needed extreme courage to keep going because others gave up?*

Kathryn had me on the edge of my seat as she shared her story. The experience happened when she was in her early 20s — something she will never forget. She was working in retail, at a clothing store located in a large Seattle-area mall. She was a talented employee and in management training at the time of the incident.

It was near closing time. She, the store's Assistant Manager, two other employees, and just a couple of customers were inside the store, when a group of five very intimidating-looking people walked in. They were dressed in hoodies and wearing ski masks over their faces. She saw the group and called her Assistant Manager's name, and when he turned, guns were drawn. The Assistant Manager immediately ran for the door, abandoning Kathryn, the other two employees, and the customers. Two of the armed persons grabbed the two other employees and led them to a back office, alerting Kathryn that somehow the gunmen already knew the layout of the store.

At one point, in the confusion, the customers who were in the store took an opportunity to flee. Kathryn could have gotten away as well at that point; however, she realized that if she left the store, she would be leaving the other two employees behind. She knew in her heart that there was no way she could do that. Because she was in management training, she had the keys to the register in her pocket. She was the only employee in the store who had the keys. Trying to keep everyone safe, Kathryn offered the keys to the robbers. Initially, they attempted to open the register without her, pushing Kathryn to the ground in the back office with the other employees. When they found that they were unable to open the register with the keys alone, they grabbed Kathryn again, demanding she open the register herself.

She opened the register as calmly as she could. Around this frightening time, she felt momentary relief when two mall security officers appeared. Unfortunately, her relief only lasted for an instant, because once the mall security guards saw the guns, the guards took off running.

There was Kathryn, left alone with the two other employees and the gunmen — who continued to threaten and scream. Since both the Assistant Manager and the mall security guards had taken off running, Kathryn suggested to the armed robbers that she could close the store doors; she offered to give them anything they wanted from the store, pleading with them not to hurt her or the other employees. Although she was frightened to the core, physically shaking, she was able to manage a calm voice, and she knew somewhere deep inside that she would be okay.

The armed robbers agreed, grabbing all the high-end items they wanted. They eventually left, taking a back exit through the employee halls, another indication that they were familiar with the workings of the mall.

Afraid to leave the store even after the robbers exited, Kathryn and the two other employees waited for the police to arrive. It took nearly forty minutes from the time when the ordeal began until law enforcement arrived. Following this harrowing experience, Kathryn continued to work for the company for about five more years. She always stayed aware of her surroundings, especially around closing time.

Kathryn credits her parents for the bravery she showed that day. When she realized that she had to lead because others gave up, her focus was always on keeping the other employees safe. This was a principle taught to her by her parents. She was raised by the most loving parents — people who always lent a helping hand whenever a need arose. She just never even considered it an option not to help someone or to leave behind a person in need.

# *Journal*

*Today's date is:*

---------------------------------------------------------------

*Journal prompt: Was there a time in your life when you needed extreme courage to keep going because others gave up?*

---------------------------------------------------------------

---------------------------------------------------------------

---------------------------------------------------------------

---------------------------------------------------------------

---------------------------------------------------------------

---------------------------------------------------------------

---------------------------------------------------------------

---------------------------------------------------------------

---------------------------------------------------------------

---------------------------------------------------------------

---------------------------------------------------------------

---------------------------------------------------------------

---------------------------------------------------------------

# Day 36

## What is the hardest thing you ever had to do?

Christi
Born: Santa Rosa, California
Headstone: Wherever you go — no matter what the weather —
bring your own sunshine

Christi and I met just weeks before our date. She approached me at a girlfriend's fiftieth birthday party and introduced herself. Her energy and welcoming smile made us instant friends. She made me feel special by simply saying, "I wanted to meet you because I've heard such great things about you." It was truly the warmest greeting I have ever received. The way she made me feel in that introduction set the tone for our friendship. It reminds me not to be afraid of approaching someone and simply saying, "I've wanted to meet you."

*Day 36: What is the hardest thing you ever had to do?*

Christi has had her fair share of life challenges, including the fact that she was struck by a personal watercraft a mere three weeks after giving birth to her daughter. On that day she was hospitalized in serious condition with a collapsed lung and multiple rib fractures. As harrowing as that was, she said, and as difficult as the physical recovery was, it isn't the hardest thing she ever had to do.

Anyone who knows Christi would describe her as friendly and outgoing. At a very young age, she decided she was going to experience life to the fullest, which meant being open to meeting people everywhere life took her. Because Christi has such incredible energy that brings people in with her smile and easy conversation, I asked if her parents are as socially outgoing as she is.

Christi explained that she was raised in a home filled with love. She described her mom and dad with incredible warmth and pride. Her parents were high school sweethearts who survived his Vietnam deployment (he won two Purple Hearts). Her dad is a true American hero. While they are both more reserved than she is, they provided her with a solid foundation. They gave her the confidence to move through the world with joy.

Christi loves to travel. She and her husband have passed this love of travel down to their children. With her adventurous spirit, it was not surprising that she took the opportunity to study abroad when she was a college coed. As a French language major at the University of Washington, she chose to study in Avignon, France. Avignon happens to be the only city outside of the Vatican where the popes had lived, which occurred from 1309 to 1377. She describes Avignon as a city surrounded by a wall which, ideally, you want to reside inside of, because this is where the culture of the city comes to life. The homes located inside the wall are those of families who have lived in the city for many generations.

She happened to be placed with a family that resided *outside* the wall, however, in government housing. Most of the neighborhood was Muslim, and no other young Catholic American women resided there. She definitely stuck out like a sore thumb — not just because of her appearance, but also because of the way she dressed and carried herself. An avid runner, she ran daily because it was the only form of exercise readily available during her stay. Unfortunately, she received shouts of disapproval and even had bottle caps thrown at her as she ran. When she walked the four miles to her school each day, she had to endure the same sort of harassment. Alas, the family she stayed with did not attempt to introduce her to their culture; they didn't make an effort to help her feel more welcome.

She felt very alone. This was the early 1990s. Cell phones weren't popular, international calls were very expensive, and letters took a week to arrive to and from the States. Fortunately, given her outgoing nature, she was finally able to connect with two other women who were also exchange students. Together, the three of them decided they would travel every other weekend to explore Europe together.

One of these travel weekends was to Spain, from which a chance meeting would change Christi's life forever.

While in Europe, whenever she could, she chose to speak French rather than English. When she and the other two exchange students travelled together, even to countries outside of France such as Spain, Christi communicated to the locals in French. She was the person in the group who did most of the communicating with locals — not because her language skills were necessarily that much better than her two companions, but because she was committed to not missing the opportunity to become as fluent in conversational French as she could.

As it usually happens, being open to speaking to others paid off. While the three exchange students were travelling through Spain, they saw a friendly family, and Christi asked them to take a photo of the three of them. After taking the photo and speaking with Christi and her friends, the family asked the trio if they'd like a tour around Barcelona. The three spent a lively afternoon with them, and the family asked if Christi and her friends would like to join them for dinner at their home. Not sure it was the wisest choice but also feeling very comfortable and welcomed by this family, they accepted their gracious invitation. Extra places were set for them at a grand table prepared by the family's cook and served delightfully by their staff. The meal was not only beautifully served, but the conversation flowed, despite the language challenges.

When Christi arrived back in the States, she developed her photos and sent a few of them with a thank-you note to the family in Spain for the hospitality they'd shown to her and her friends. Christi continued corresponding with the family, and later received an offer to join them upon graduation from college, as their au pair. The family had historically hired European English-speaking au pairs for their daughter, but they loved Christi so much that for the first time they thought having an American au pair would be perfect. Christi realized that this was an opportunity for her to travel and have an amazing experience in Spain for a year, so she jumped at the chance. She ended up having the best experience — as they quickly became her second family.

Through the years, she has stayed in touch with her second family — including with their daughter who recently got married this past year. Christi attended the wedding, which was held in a beautiful castle on a Spanish mountainside. Christi was the only former au pair who had been invited to attend — a testament to just how closely and perfectly matched she was to this family.

Because Christi stuck it out through the hardest thing she ever had to do — living with a family in a place where she did not fit in and felt utterly alone — her creativity and openness led to a chance meeting with a wonderful family, people who literally changed her life.

Christi's story reminds me that the Universe's timing is always perfect. When we think that things aren't going our way, often we find that the Universe knows better. We may not realize it at the time, but the Universe puts us in a place where we need to be because of the experiences we are going to have.

Albert Einstein once posed the question, "Is this a friendly universe or is this a hostile universe?"

Once we decide that the Universe is our friend, we can find comfort in knowing that even during the hardest times in our life, we're being led to something amazing.

# Journal

*Today's date is:*

----------------------------------------

*Journal prompt: What is the hardest thing you ever had to do?*

----------------------------------------

----------------------------------------

----------------------------------------

----------------------------------------

----------------------------------------

----------------------------------------

----------------------------------------

----------------------------------------

----------------------------------------

----------------------------------------

----------------------------------------

----------------------------------------

----------------------------------------

----------------------------------------

"If life didn't have obstacles to overcome, it would be boring — and boring is torture."
— Shari Leid

# Day 37

## If you had to evacuate your house due to a fire, what three things would you take?

Athina
Born: Powell River, British Columbia, Canada
Headstone: Eternally devoted to her children and husband

I met Athina through her amazing floral designs (www.athinaflora.
com). Our mutual girlfriend, who is also one of Athina's floral
clients and the owner of a high-end event-planning business,
recommended Athina to me. Because our mutual friend has a keen
artistic sense and impeccable style, I knew her recommendation
would be excellent. What I didn't realize is that not only was
I meeting a talented floral designer, but I was also making an
extraordinary new friend.

*Day 37: If you had to evacuate your house due to a fire, what three things
would you take?*

Without hesitation and very easily, Athina listed the three items she would grab before anything else:

1. First, she would take her maternal grandmother's baking pan. Athina's mother and father immigrated to Canada from Greece, meeting and falling in love in Canada. While her immediate family was not able to travel to Greece to visit extended family when Athina was a young child, they were able to travel as a family when Athina and her brothers were a little older. She remembers how happy her grandmother was to have the family visit.

   On one of their first family trips to Greece, before leaving to return home to Canada, her grandmother insisted that Athina's mom take something. Despite her mom's protests, exclaiming that she didn't need anything, her grandmother insisted and gave her a large oval metal pan. Athina remembers her grandmother using the pan for wonderful, lively family meals in Greece — a tradition her mom continued upon returning home to Canada, and eventually she passed the pan on to Athina. Every holiday and during regular family meals, Athina brings out the pan. When she uses it, she thinks of her grandmother and her mother. While preparing a meal is always an act of love, preparing it in a pan so rich in family history and love makes the food prepared in it extra special.

2. Second, she would take her mom's Saint Fevronia icon. Saint Fevronia is the patron saint of marriage and family as well as a symbol of love and fidelity. The icon, which is a special piece of art, was given to Athina by her mom — who is

named Fevronia — on her wedding day. It was hand-painted by monks at a seminary in Greece. I learned from Athina that in most traditional households in Greece, there are walls or areas of the house dedicated to a collection of various icons. Athina hangs only the one icon, her beloved St. Fevronia icon. She feels her mother's love every time she walks by it.

3.   Athina has a daughter and son who are her world. Before each of them was born, she carefully chose their going-home outfits. These are the first outfits they ever wore outside of the hospital room. Not only were the outfits darling, but they also represent one of her first acts as a mother, to keep her children safe and warm. In case of fire, she would be sure to take these keepsake outfits with her.

Athina also noted that she never takes off her wedding ring. She knows that the symbol of her marriage is always with her.

The three things that mean the most to her are the things that keep her grounded. Family has always been the most important thing for Athina. The three things she chose, which would not be worth much to anyone else, mean the world to her. Thinking about the items Athina chose — items that have no actual monetary value but are priceless — reminds me of what is truly essential in life: the people you love and cherish.

# Journal

*Today's date is:*

-------------------------------------------------------------------

*Journal prompt: If you had to evacuate your house due to a fire, what three things would you take?*

-------------------------------------------------------------------

-------------------------------------------------------------------

-------------------------------------------------------------------

-------------------------------------------------------------------

-------------------------------------------------------------------

-------------------------------------------------------------------

-------------------------------------------------------------------

-------------------------------------------------------------------

-------------------------------------------------------------------

-------------------------------------------------------------------

-------------------------------------------------------------------

-------------------------------------------------------------------

-------------------------------------------------------------------

-------------------------------------------------------------------

-------------------------------------------------------------------

"Friendship is one of the best gifts of life."

— Shari Leid

# Day 38

## If you had to evacuate your house because of a devastating earthquake, what three things would you take?

Trish
Born: Whittier, California
Headstone: Bury me with a martini up,
with an olive on the side.

Trish and I met at a friend's home. We are fortunate to have many great girlfriends in common, which made our meeting inevitable. I found that Trish meets new people as if they were old friends. She is quick to invite someone into a conversation. She can make even the most socially shy person feel at home in a group because of her fun and friendly welcoming nature.

*Day 38: If you had to evacuate your house because of a devastating earthquake, what three things would you take?*

This question hit close to home for Trish, who was living in San Francisco in 1989 during the 6.9-magnitude Loma Prieta earthquake — which resulted in sixty-four deaths and 3,757 injuries. Damage was heavy in the Marina District of San Francisco, where Trish was living at the time. She was inside her apartment during the quake, and after the rumblings subsided, she stepped out of her building and was shocked to see that the apartment building across the street had fallen and the streets in front of her had buckled.

The world was quite different in 1989. Cell phones were basically only available to the wealthy, who could install them in their cars. And even then, they were quite rare to find. Email and the internet were still a decade away from becoming readily available. Fortunately, Trish's brother lived nearby, and they had made plans to meet up that day. They were relieved to be able to locate one another; but they were not able to reach their parents to tell them that they were safe, because their parents resided across the Bay Bridge — which had collapsed. Thankfully, Trish and her brother eventually were able to connect with their parents. They'd been very worried because the news had been showing that the Marina District was ablaze.

Trish was dating a man (who is now her husband) whom she had planned to surprise by showing up at his birthday party, which was being held in Seattle — on the day after the earthquake happened. Deciding that she would travel anyway as planned, she was allowed into her apartment by a police escort to grab some items. She was given only fifteen minutes to fill a suitcase. She took her favorite pants — which she describes as "these amazing leather pants"; her jewelry; a few other clothing items; and her camera. She took only items that she knew she needed to get her through the next few weeks.

As *bad luck* would have it, the airline lost Trish's luggage, and it was never to be recovered. If you had asked her young thirty-something self before the earthquake, she may have described those items as things that would have devastated her if ever they were lost. But she realized that, although she sure did miss those amazing leather pants, she could live without even those items that she absolutely loved.

Thinking about what she would grab all these years later given the same situation, Trish said that the things she would grab are not too different from what she chose back then. She would take her clothes and jewelry, her phone, and any medication that was needed. Her items are not sentimental in nature, but practical items that would allow her to survive and move forward.

And that's who Trish is. She is someone who enjoys the present and looks forward to the future. I'm not surprised that when limited to just three items, the three she thought of were not sentimental keepsakes but rather items that would allow her to avoid skipping a beat or losing a moment to be present — so that she could keep enjoying life as it happens.

# Journal

*Today's date is:*

---

*Journal prompt: If you had to evacuate your house because of a devastating earthquake, what three things would you take?*

---

"Instead of holding your loved ones close, see what happens when you let them soar."
— Shari Leid

# *Day 39*

# What is more important: justice or forgiveness?

Deci
Born: Newburg, New York
Headstone: A friend to all

I met Deci years ago at a couple's night out. At the time, both of my kids were attending a neighborhood Montessori preschool, and one of Deci's close friends was a parent at that same school. In addition to being a mom to two active preschoolers, I was actively practicing law as a solo practitioner in downtown Seattle. My law firm sponsored a local comedy show and I hosted a table at the show for a parents' night out. Deci's girlfriend invited her and her husband (her fiancé at the time) to join us at the comedy show. We've been friends ever since.

*Day 39: What is more important: justice or forgiveness?*

*Justice: the maintenance or administration of what is just, especially by the impartial adjustment of conflicting claims or the assignment of merited rewards or punishments.*

*Forgive*: *to cease to feel resentment against an offender.*

Deci is friendly and outgoing. She is someone who can sit down next to anyone and easily talk to that person — she's already a friend. After our initial meeting at the comedy club, I invited Deci to several parties at my home. We've been together at these large gatherings on several occasions, which has been fun. However, I've really appreciated that the last two times we've been together it has been just the two of us, giving us the opportunity to have great conversations.

Our date for this book occurred on the heels of former police officer Derek Chauvin's conviction for the murder of George Floyd. Although Deci and I didn't discuss the case, I couldn't help but think about the conviction as we began our conversation around my question for her. While the news stations were reporting that the prevailing public sentiment was that justice was served in the conviction of Chauvin, I couldn't help but wonder if this verdict would bring the much-needed healing to the Black community. Would healing need more than justice? Would it take forgiveness for the healing to begin?

As these thoughts about the Chauvin trial danced in my head, Deci, without hesitation, shared with me that she believes that forgiveness is more important than justice. She further explained that she believes that forgiveness is most important to the person doing the forgiving, and less important for the person receiving the forgiveness. She explained that being able to forgive someone who has deeply angered or hurt you is not at all easy, but she strongly believes that it is the only way to heal and move forward.

She came to this belief in part due to her own life experiences. Something that had a profound effect on her was a painful experience that she endured as a child. She realized that after being deeply betrayed and hurt by a mentally unstable older family member, for her to be able to move forward and to live the life she wanted for herself, she would have to forgive. It didn't matter if the person received justice or not; if she couldn't forgive this person in her heart, she knew she would be trapped in anger. Forgiveness gave her the freedom to live fully as she let go of the anger and pain.

I love Deci's focus on the power that forgiveness has on the person who is doing the forgiving. While you can't always choose what happens to you, you can always choose your response and your actions going forward. By forgiving, you're taking control of the situation and steering your own life. While it can mean a lot if you find that the person you're forgiving accepts and cares about the forgiveness you're extending, that really isn't what matters. What matters is what you feel in your heart — which will give you the strength to both heal and move on. Healing comes from within. It can't come from another person. Therefore, forgiveness is most vital for the person granting the forgiveness.

While both justice and forgiveness are important for moving forward into a better future, it is the act of being able to forgive that gives freedom to the one who was wronged.

# Journal

*Today's date is:*

_____

*Journal prompt: What is more important: justice or forgiveness?*

_____

_____

_____

_____

_____

_____

_____

_____

_____

_____

_____

_____

_____

_____

"Forgiving is the hardest thing I've ever had to do, even harder than running — and I hate running!"

— Shari Leid

# Day 40

## What do you appreciate about your life right now? Why?

Karen
Born: Renton, Washington
Headstone: Her love continues to shine brightly in those she loved

K aren and I met through our work with a local non-profit whose goal is to help women obtain a livable wage through educational grants and services. We sat on the same board for nearly a year, and during that time, Karen switched careers. She is now a certified life coach (www.karenpatricelli.com). We had spoken about coaching before, and she ended up choosing the same school I attended — iPEC Coaching, a school with a fabulous success record, certified by the International Coaching Federation. It was great for us to meet in person for this date. Because of the nature of this project, I knew our friendship would automatically deepen, because relationships always become richer when we sit down and take the time to hear each other's story.

*Day 40*: *What do you appreciate about your life right now? Why?*

Karen loves where her life is right now. It is remarkable that she is so happy with where her life is today, because it took a few unexpected twists and turns to get here. After going through a difficult divorce and getting back to a feeling of stability in her new role as a single mom, Karen's world was rocked by covid-19. Not only was the pandemic turning the world upside down, but she was blindsided by an unexpected layoff from her place of employment — where she had worked for over seventeen years. To add additional sting to the shock of being furloughed, the news was delivered by a close friend who was also a co-worker. And after about five months, the furlough turned into a permanent job loss. So, there she was, a single mom in her late fifties, amidst a pandemic and unemployed.

Then, beauty from the chaos started to emerge. Karen took a serious look at who she was and where she wanted to spend her energy. She had already been thinking about her career — and what living a life filled with intention and purpose looked like for her. She was on a path towards self-discovery, so losing her job simply propelled her forward. While she thought she liked her job, she realized that what she really had enjoyed was the people she worked with, more than the work itself. She decided to enroll in coaching school to obtain a professional coaching certification — in part to help her become a more effective parent but also to dive even deeper into self-discovery. She knew that her career experience could help others who were transitioning in their careers or building a business.

As the weeks progressed, she noticed that she was able to enjoy life just a little bit more, because she wasn't tied to a work schedule dictated by someone else. She began to live her life by her own design. She even noticed that for the first time in a long time, her mind was not preoccupied. She started to notice that even the sound of her children's laughter was something she could pause to appreciate. By changing her mindset, Karen was able to see the boundless opportunities that came from being thrown life's curveball.

What initially seemed like a giant obstacle turned out to be a detour that took Karen to a better place. She is currently the happiest she has ever been.

# Journal

Today's date is:

------------------------------------------------------------

Journal prompt: *What do you appreciate about your life right now? Why?*

------------------------------------------------------------

------------------------------------------------------------

------------------------------------------------------------

------------------------------------------------------------

------------------------------------------------------------

------------------------------------------------------------

------------------------------------------------------------

------------------------------------------------------------

------------------------------------------------------------

------------------------------------------------------------

------------------------------------------------------------

------------------------------------------------------------

------------------------------------------------------------

------------------------------------------------------------

"My life is imperfectly perfect."
— Shari Leid

# Day 41

## What do you think is the meaning of life?

Anne Marie
Born: Shoreline, Washington
Headstone: Here lies Anne Marie — a good wife, mother, and friend. You were never hungry when you were with her.

Approximately seven years ago, my husband and I attended our city's annual Chamber auction, where we bid on and won a chef's wine-paired dinner party at our home for eight guests, donated and prepared by Anne Marie (www.chefannemarie.com). We invited my husband's college friends and their wives over for a very fun and memorable evening. That night was the first night of many events at our home that Anne Marie made special with her talent in the kitchen, creating the perfect experiences for our guests.

*Day 41: What do you think is the meaning of life?*

Speaking with Anne Marie reminded me once again of why I love these *Friendship* conversations. Although we've known each other for several years and have exchanged countless emails and texts, we've never taken the time to speak to each other on a personal level. Anne Marie has created so many fabulous meals for my friends and family — events which will never be forgotten. A countless number of people have met and become friends while attending these events in my home — socializing while enjoying the special meals that she has created.

I am grateful to have had the opportunity during the writing of this book to finally take the time to share with her how much she has impacted not just my life but the lives of so many who have come into my home and enjoyed her culinary creations.

Anne Marie believes that the meaning of life comes down to relationships. I fully agree with her. She shared with me that in her life she has loved and lost. She has been wealthy and poor. She has celebrated and grieved. Her father passed away while she was still in high school, and then she lost her mom just a few short years later, at the tender age of twenty-one. She became a first-time mom at only twenty-two. Then came the painful unimaginable loss of two children, and a marriage that dissolved. But she found a new love and a wonderful second marriage. She is building a business and rebuilding her life. Anne Marie has lived a life of profound ups and downs — a winding journey, always filled with growth. Through it all, she has come to believe that the meaning of life is not about acquiring material possessions or titles but about nurturing and enjoying relationships.

This belief brings us to the importance that sharing a meal plays in building relationships. As Anne Marie explained, food is the second-largest monthly expense that everyone has. The kitchen is the center of the home. It is where families and friends come together. It doesn't matter our race, political beliefs, religious beliefs, sexual orientation, or gender — food brings us together.

One of Anne Marie's first memories of bringing people together with the food she created was when her father passed away. She was only seventeen years of age when she was pulled out of class and told that her father had died. When the news of her father's death became known, friends and family members filled her home. She remembers wanting to help her mother, who was busy greeting all the guests. So, without consulting her, Anne Marie made a large spaghetti meal to feed everyone. To her surprise, the guests were amazed that at just seventeen, she had prepared dinner for the entire house. It was her way of not only taking care of her mom, but also of caring for all the people who came to visit.

From that young age, Anne Marie witnessed the power that sharing food has in building relationships — and even providing comfort and showing love. One of her missions is to help people feel comfortable in the kitchen so they can also feel the love and connection that comes from preparing a meal to share with family and friends. She began a program called Kitchen Competent — an online course in which she shares basic food and kitchen knowledge. In the class she emphasizes that once you feel competent with the basics, you can do anything in the kitchen.

If you look up inspirational quotes about food, often you will also find the word *love*.

Believing that the most important thing in life is the relationships we have, Anne Marie is helping to create those relationships through her gift as a chef, which she happily imparts to others. One of her favorite sayings is, "A gift is not a gift until it is given."

# Journal

*Today's date is:*

---

*Journal prompt: What do you think is the meaning of life?*

---

---

---

---

---

---

---

---

---

---

---

---

---

---

"I want to laugh one billion times more than cry during this lifetime — that is my goal."
— Shari Leid

# Ask Yourself This

## Today:
## Shari's Own Reflections

1. *When you're down, what makes you feel better?* Journaling, listening to a positive podcast, intentional breathing, and gathering of my thoughts to regain perspective — these all feel very healing for me. I find it is helpful for me to look for the learning points in my experience. This process allows me to shift my energy from feeling down to understanding, acceptance, and moving forward with more positive energy.

2. *What do you complain about more than anything else?* My internet connection.

3. *Was there a time in your life when you needed extreme courage to keep going because others gave up?* While I can't (thankfully) think of a situation where extreme courage was required and others around me gave up, I can think of many situations where I needed courage. I am reminded of the number of physical challenges that I've experienced, some of which brought

on bouts of profound sadness. It was particularly hard for me to stand tall when I wanted to shut down and hide in my early 20s after experiencing significant facial lacerations that required multiple scar-revision surgeries following a near-fatal automobile accident. It required courage for me, a self-conscious twenty-two-year-old, to continue to attend college and law school classes while receiving side glances as each revision surgery brought on a round of "it has to get bad to get good" visual scar healing. Reflecting on this question reminds me of how fortunate I am to be surrounded by strong friends and family members who not only support me but also do not give up when life throws curveballs.

4.  *What is the hardest thing you ever had to do?* Losing my dad, who died suddenly of a heart attack, was the hardest thing I've ever had to go through. Losing my dad was what I feared since childhood. He was forty-eight when he adopted me, and it was considered very old — to become a dad at that age — in the 1970s. He was the age of my friends' grandparents, so I was always aware of how old he was. When my greatest fear came true, it destroyed me. He died a month after my thirty-first birthday — on the morning of my mom's birthday — collapsing onto their bedroom floor. It took me a solid three years to recover from feeling lost without him. Six months after he died, my husband and I brought home our adopted daughter from China. Fourteen months after he died, I gave birth to our son. Having my children saved me from greater despair; but in hindsight, I really could have benefited from grief counseling to help me process the

profound loss and sadness that I felt for those three years following his sudden death.

5.   *If you had to evacuate your house due to a fire, what three things would you take?* 1) Cell phone; 2) computer; and 3) something of my dad's that has his handwriting on it — maybe a poem that he wrote for me. After he retired, he began writing poems for friends and family on their birthdays. At the time it seemed like a fun hobby. Now I feel his poems were a gift of love. The beauty of them is that I find one occasionally — in an album, a file, or a box — and when I do, it feels like a surprise hug from heaven.

6.   *If you had to evacuate your house because of a devastating earthquake, what three things would you take?* I realize that an earthquake can be just as destructive as a fire — but perhaps naively I feel like I could return home after a quake to recover items that matter to me. Therefore, my focus would be more on what I'd need to survive for the next twenty-four hours. 1) I would take my phone; 2) my wallet; and 3) my travel kit, which is always filled with make-up and basic toiletries.

7.   *What is more important: justice or forgiveness?* When I was younger, I would have answered, *justice* without thinking twice. I used to react to stress and conflict by immediately going into *fight mode*. My mentality was, "They need to pay" or "They get what they deserve." My views on justice and forgiveness have completely shifted as I've gotten older. I now believe that although difficult, forgiveness is one of the most powerful

human acts there is. In my opinion, forgiveness is much more important and potent than justice. I believe forgiveness heals the soul and allows people to move forward. Forgiveness helps us see opportunity even in the face of adversity and sorrow.

8.  *What do you appreciate about your life right now? Why?* I appreciate that I'm alive. Each year, on my birthday, I say a prayer of thanks for having the opportunity to live the past year, and to share joy in the possibilities of the year to come — knowing that my work on Earth is not finished. I love being in my 50s. This is a decade in which I'm more confident than I was in decades past. I'm not affected by fear of judgment, which held me hostage in my early adult life.

    My favorite quote, which comes in the form of a question is, "If today were the last day of your life, would you be doing what you are doing now?" Keeping that question replaying in my mind keeps me on the right track — to enjoy my life each day to the fullest, not wasting my precious time on worry, anger, or regret!

9.  *What do you think is the meaning of life?* To collectively learn from one another through experience and conversation. Also, I believe we have each been given unique gifts and talents, and with them we must take responsibility to support and care for our communities and for the world at large.

# Ask Yourself This

## Inspiration and Motivation

# Day 42

## What's your favorite quotation?

Dana

Born: New York City

Headstone: Little Miss Sunshine [*a loving nickname from childhood*]

Dana and I met while in costume, and it wouldn't be the last time we would find ourselves together donning costumes. In fact, I think that in our five years of friendship, we've probably been at themed costume events nearly half of the number of times we've been together. Our initial meeting was at a girlfriend's large outdoor Halloween party, followed by two holiday-themed large cookie-exchange parties at my home; and then there was my fiftieth birthday party, for which we dressed in 80s prom attire. I love a girl who can dress silly for the sake of carrying out a party theme. And I have always said that the thing I love the most about costume or theme parties is that everyone looks equally silly — so it's easier to meet new friends without judgment.

*Day 42: What's your favorite quotation?*

Dana teaches kindergarteners and first-graders. I still remember my kindergarten and first-grade teachers. These were the teachers who set the tone for the rest of my schooling. They shaped who I believed myself to be as a student and life-long learner. They made school into something I looked forward to and wanted to be a part of. I remember feeling encouraged by my teachers to strive for more knowledge. They made me feel like I could accomplish anything. Now that I look back, I think of how lucky I was to have had such outstanding teachers to kick off my beginning educational years.

How fortunate Dana's students are to have the same experience as I did: a teacher who really believes in them, who is setting the tone for the rest of their careers as life-long learners. I wonder how many students have come through her classroom, how many young lives she has touched, and the ripple effect that her influence has had on these children and on the communities they will become members of.

Dana shared the following three quotes, which Dana sees as life's guideposts:

*"Life is a series of who you know, not what you know."* This quote is from Bob Lowy, Dana's dad. I love that. She has a close relationship with her father, like what I had with my own dad. As we spoke, seeing the admiration she has for him made me feel as if I were being hugged by my own dad, whom I miss dearly. Another similarity that we share is that Dana, like me, is adopted. Dana's face lit up as she talked — not only about her dad, but also about her family, which includes her mom and her sister, who is also an adoptee.

Her dad was a Human Resources professional. He is someone who brings the energy of a room up several notches when he walks in. He makes friends easily, and in Dana's words, "he knows everyone, and everyone knows him." His quote embodies what he believes in and practices: recognizing the importance of relationships, the importance of friendships, and the importance of connections. In other words, it doesn't matter if you know everything about baseball, if you have no one to go to the game with. I imagine he credits much of his success to understanding the field of Human Resources — keeping up on laws, regulations, and standards of practice — but also, he would credit the importance of the relationships that he's made and maintained throughout his life.

Dana had a second quote to share — one that she has not only loved for the past twenty years, but it is also something she shares with her students. She has this quote hanging in her classroom because she has made it the classroom motto: *"Be kind. No exceptions."* Dana teaches her young students that even during a disagreement, they can still be kind. As Dana points out, you never know someone's story — what they've been through — so processing your way through a disagreement can occur much more effectively when communication is done with kindness. Therefore, she adheres to this quote as a guide for how her students are to treat their classmates.

The last quote she shared with me is one that has taken center stage for her during the year that we met for this discussion: *"Life begins at the end of your comfort zone."* We met during Dana's year of moving towards fifty. To honor this milestone birthday, she created a list of fifty things that she will accomplish throughout the year. Many of the items are things that sit outside of her comfort zone. Personally, as a mindset coach specializing in coaching women who are in their tricky middle years, I find time and time again that the limits we think we have are in fact limits that are self-imposed. When we realize this, we can challenge ourselves to push those so that we can live the life of our dreams.

Inspirational quotes can take on a personal meaning. They can become a daily mantra, and a guiding light. These quotes that Dana shared aren't mere words to repeat; they can carve out a way of life.

# Journal

*Today's date is:*

---

*What's your favorite quotation?*

---

# Day 43

## What lessons did you learn this past year, and how have you grown and improved?

Kimberly
Born: Seattle
Headstone: The sun shined brighter because she made an impact

I can't be quite sure, but Kimberly and I first met briefly at either a girlfriend's birthday party or at a fundraising event for the Fred Hutch Cancer Research Institute. Both were brief meetings which happened around the same time.

On several occasions before meeting Kimberly, various friends had said, "I can't believe you don't know Kimberly. You must know Kimberly."

And looking at all the mutual friends that we do have, and since both of us grew up in the same city, it is a surprise that we never met until just two years ago. While I admittedly know a lot of people in our city, Kimberly seems to know everyone.

*Day 43: What lessons did you learn this past year, and how have you grown and improved?*

Kimberly is the founder and CEO of FashWire (www.fashwire.com) and GlossWire (www.glosswire.com) — global marketplaces offering one-stop solutions for consumers to organically discover fashion and beauty. She connects brands and creators to consumers by leveraging technology to engage shoppers across all channels.

Prior to launching FashWire in 2018, Kimberly, who previously worked in the tech world, was a successful small brick-and-mortar business owner, running a popular and trendy fashion boutique in Seattle. Deciding to jump back into the tech world as a founder of FashWire was certainly a big career leap — working with investors, a board, a team of employees and contractors, and learning the ins and outs of her new tech platform and online fashion community. She also jumped into communicating with brands, designers, consumers, and investors on a global scale. While huge company and professional growth happened in a very short period, one of the most important assets came in the form of a personal epiphany when the covid-19 pandemic hit.

A self-described Type-A personality, Kimberly's default comfort level has always been to control every aspect of a project. Her attention to detail, strong work ethic, and ability to hold her vision are the elements that have made her successful. I didn't ask Kimberly how many hours per week she was logging in prior to the pandemic, but I'm sure with all the travel she was doing for her business, the time she logged in reached well over the standard forty hours. Before the pandemic, she frequently travelled from L.A. to New York, as well as internationally to fashion meccas such as London and Berlin. The fashion trade shows were the bread and butter of her business — making connections with designers, scouting talent, and reaching investors. Overnight, fashion shows and travel came to a sudden stop. Kimberly found herself at the mercy of the ever-changing pandemic regulations, and she had to pivot.

When I asked Kimberly my question, her answer was, "I learned to develop trust."

Often, life's timing is perfect. Just before the pandemic really began to affect business, Kimberly had just begun to work on developing more trust, realizing that she did not need to control every single detail of her business. The business operations that were suddenly halted due to the pandemic simply fast-forwarded the path that she was already on. She made a commitment to trusting that she'd put the right team together and that she could solve any problem that came her way.

Once she made an affirmative decision to trust, the answers and options started to flow. She felt her body relax and her mind was free from worry, which allowed her to face the constantly changing policies and practices brought on by the pandemic with an ease that she hadn't had before. She gave her team more latitude in their decision-making and implementation of ideas. She supported their growth as leaders, collectively and individually, and they proudly rose to the challenge. She also noticed that putting trust in her team was contagious. Her team, while noticing the change in her leadership style, started to relax and trust in themselves and each other — even more than they had prior to covid-19.

They were all accustomed to using *control* more than *trust* as their means of moving towards successful outcomes. But during the pandemic Kimberly was able to ensure her team that they would still have jobs. She let them know that she was going to do everything in her power not to lay anyone off despite the constant and challenging changes in the fashion world. She also didn't waiver in her commitment to being involved in philanthropic endeavors. She continued donating ten percent of her monthly proceeds to charity. She has a great number of charities she supports on a regular basis — and even more she has supported through a special event or charity month focus. One of her favorite non-profits is an organization that is near to her heart, Cancer Cartel (www.cancercartel.com), whose mission is to provide financial resources and relief to those fighting cancer.

Kimberly's trust in her team has paid off. In recent months, she received one of the biggest compliments of her career, and it wasn't related to any of the multiple industry awards her businesses have received. Her biggest compliment came from her employees through an investor, who explained to her that he wanted to invest in her company because her employees raved to him about what an incredible person she is to work for. They gave him examples of her leadership style, telling him about the weekly team meetings in which she solicits feedback and ideas from all her employees on a regular basis. According to him, for employees to do this when Kimberly wasn't even present was a true mark of the impact she was making — not just in the business world, but also in the lives of those around her. That, he said, was someone worth investing in.

The adoption of trust as an intention has extended beyond Kimberly's work life, to her parenting style. She shared a very personal story with me about her son, who struggled with classes when his school moved to remote learning. While her son was worried that he was letting his parents down and feeling overwhelmed by his struggle, Kimberly patiently helped him break down the steps he could take so that the classes wouldn't be so overwhelming. She shared with him her trust that he would be fine. Her trust proved once again to be contagious, as he was then able to trust in his own abilities. Sure enough, he not only pulled out of the troubling spot he was in, but soon excelled in all his classes.

My clients have heard me share my belief that the Universe is a friendly place. You just need to do the work, and the Universe will meet you halfway. In other words, trust that everything will work out — and you will not just be okay, but you will thrive.

Kimberly's experience is a demonstration of what can happen when you add just a little more trust to your life — a lesson that has not only helped her grow and improve but has also helped the people around her do the same.

# Journal

*Today's date is:*

------------------------------------------------------------

*Journal prompt: What lessons did you learn this past year, and how have you grown and improved?*

------------------------------------------------------------

------------------------------------------------------------

------------------------------------------------------------

------------------------------------------------------------

------------------------------------------------------------

------------------------------------------------------------

------------------------------------------------------------

------------------------------------------------------------

------------------------------------------------------------

------------------------------------------------------------

------------------------------------------------------------

------------------------------------------------------------

------------------------------------------------------------

------------------------------------------------------------

------------------------------------------------------------

------------------------------------------------------------

"Every curveball I've been
thrown has led me to
something greater than I could
have imagined."
— Shari Leid

Every day is an opportunity to make a positive difference in someone else's life.

# Day 44

## How are you creating a life well lived?

Janel
Born: Seattle
Headstone: Love without condition because love always wins

I met Janel during the pandemic through her older sister, Stacy. When I told Stacy that one of my life's missions is to help women make connections and deepen their relationships — often through teaching them how to listen to another's personal stories — she immediately said that I must meet her sister, Janel.

*Day 44: How are you creating a life well lived?*

Janel was very excited to talk to me because of what she does for a living. She helps people tell their story. Janel runs a program launched in 2013 by The Port Gamble S'Klallam Tribe: a revolutionary new program in Washington state that takes a non-punitive approach to reentry into society from incarceration. The program puts human dignity, connection, and compassion front and center. The end goal is to give these individuals the tools they need to become contributing members of society and to embrace the possibility of a positive future — through connections, storytelling, culture, and community.

Driven by a holistic approach, the program recognizes that individual success is not one-size-fits-all. For every client, the journey begins with a risk and needs assessment, to help tailor their services and support. A Success Coach, rather than a Probation Officer, is assigned. Healing circles take place, in which the perpetrator of the crime, the victim, the law enforcement officer, and members of the community are able to meet, share their stories, offer forgiveness, and heal together. Facilitating these circles, Janel has witnessed the power of communication. She has seen first-hand the miracles that happen when we listen to one another's story.

Janel told me that if she could create a healing circle for everyone to experience, she would. The transformation of lives that she has experienced from her work has given her a life well lived. She is doing exactly what she knows she was born to do: facilitate communication and healing. From a young age, she knew she was placed here on Earth to make connections happen. Janel believes strongly that there is good in everyone. It is impossible for Janel not to see that spark of good in another person, even in someone who may have been dismissed as irredeemable.

Janel's belief is, "When you look for the good in someone, it's hard to be angry, because [in her view] the two [anger and good] can't co-exist."

During our conversation, Janel introduced me to Kay Pranis, who is a national leader in restorative justice, specializing in peacemaking circles. She has been working with these healing circles since 1996. She emphasizes that teachers come from everywhere, which is something that Janel witnesses on a day-to-day basis — seeing it happen with people from all walks of life. While it is easy to recognize the healing that a victim needs, we often overlook the healing that needs to occur for the person who committed the crime. If the perpetrator is to become a member of society again, healing must happen on both sides.

My *Friendship* series is about listening to my girlfriends' stories, asking questions that I have never asked, and thus getting to know my friends on a deeper level. It mirrors the work Janel does in the justice system. In each conversation, we learn something new, which allows us to understand at a greater level how the unique life experiences that we each have shape our beliefs and actions.

From this practice, I have also learned, similar to Janel's belief, that there is good in everyone. To discover it is just a matter of listening to someone else's story. Through the act of listening, we find our human connection.

# Journal

*Today's date is:*

------------------------------------------------------------

*Journal prompt: How are you creating a life well lived?*

------------------------------------------------------------

------------------------------------------------------------

------------------------------------------------------------

------------------------------------------------------------

------------------------------------------------------------

------------------------------------------------------------

------------------------------------------------------------

------------------------------------------------------------

------------------------------------------------------------

------------------------------------------------------------

------------------------------------------------------------

------------------------------------------------------------

------------------------------------------------------------

------------------------------------------------------------

------------------------------------------------------------

"You can live a life by design and trust that the Universe has a plan. The two are not mutually exclusive."
— Shari Leid

# Day 45

## What song best describes
## your life?

Alane
Born: Seattle
Headstone: She was a squirrely kind of girl

I have known Alane and her sister, Lyanne (Day 32), my entire life. We grew up attending the same church — a church I attended through high school and sporadically in my early adult life before I chose to leave organized religion. Alane, like her sister, is still active in the church with many close friends and family who are also active members. We not only attended the same church as children, but our childhood homes were located just a ten-minute drive away from each other.

As a child, I had many playdates with both her and her sister on a regular basis. I remember once her mom saying she liked having me over because I was able to play with both girls together, without leaving one of them out. I never thought about it until now, but it is a trait I think I still naturally carry — easily being able to include an entire group despite age or background. When we were kids, I rarely called Alane by her given name, but rather used her nickname, *Mushi*, which she still goes by among her family and close friends. Meaning *bug* in Japanese, it's a nickname she was given because of the way she crawled quickly on the floor as a baby.

Date 45: *What song best describes your life?*

The song that best describes Alane's life is *Famous For (I Believe)* by Christian contemporary artist Tauren Wells. I had never heard of the artist or the song, and I looked forward to listening to it and reading the lyrics following our meeting.

Just looking at the title of the song and the question I asked, you would think Alane was talking about being famous herself. However, after speaking with Alane and having a chance to actually listen to the song, I realize now that the song is about asking God to do what He is famous for. The song's lyrics remind Alane of the type of relationship she has with God and serve as a guidepost for Alane's Christian faith, reminding her to have courage to move through life without fear because of her faith in God.

It appears Alane is not alone in finding inspiration from the song. When I found it on YouTube, the version I listened to had 1.3K comments, including mentions from many individuals who said that they listen to this song daily. *Famous For (I Believe)* inspires many people to have faith as they walk through some of life's toughest challenges. And now that I am aware of the song, I recognize it being played relatively often during workouts through my at-home Mirror Fitness on-demand classes.

Talking to Alane prompted me to look at one of my favorite songs, *Beyond* by Leon Bridges, to see its comments on YouTube. I found comments like those left in the comments section of Alane's favorite song — even though the genre and subject matter differ. Both songs are inspirational to many listeners.

A few years ago, I wrote a personal mission statement, which sits on my bedstand. I think everyone should write one. After my discussion with Alane, I think that in addition to writing a mission statement, we should also choose an anthem — a song that inspires you.

What tune do you choose? Find a song that makes you feel good and urges you to sing along (whether you can sing on key or not). Recognize why the song speaks to you. Pinpoint what about it inspires you. Along with your personal mission statement, as your daily meditation you can incorporate your favorite song. You'll find that it's hard to be sad or angry while you're singing and dancing along.

# Journal

*Today's date is:*

--------------------------------------------------------------

*Journal prompt: What song best describes your life?*

--------------------------------------------------------------

--------------------------------------------------------------

--------------------------------------------------------------

--------------------------------------------------------------

--------------------------------------------------------------

--------------------------------------------------------------

--------------------------------------------------------------

--------------------------------------------------------------

--------------------------------------------------------------

--------------------------------------------------------------

--------------------------------------------------------------

--------------------------------------------------------------

--------------------------------------------------------------

--------------------------------------------------------------

--------------------------------------------------------------

"I have different theme songs for different times of my life. The older I get, the happier the songs become."
— Shari Leid

# Day 46

## If you had to write a book, what would you write about?

Stacy
Born: Bellevue, Washington
Headstone: Kind. . .Thoughtful. . .Faithful

I met Stacy through a mutual girlfriend who throws the most fabulous parties — a woman who has brought many amazing women into my life. We met about five years ago, but the opportunity to talk without the distraction that comes with larger gatherings has been rare. So, it was especially great to have this precious time for us to sit down to chat. Stacy and her husband are owners of one of the most beautiful tasting rooms and event spaces in Woodinville, Washington called Chateau Lill (www.chateaulill.com). It is the spot where I send all of my out-of-town friends to visit when they ask for a wine-tasting experience. The gorgeous grounds come complete with the opportunity to visit the resident alpacas.

*Day 46: If you had to write a book, what would you write about?*

Stacy has never thought of writing a book. Being asked to think about this question made her really ponder what message is so important to her that it would be worth sharing in a book. I'm not surprised that Stacy's immediate focus was on the positive difference she would want her book to make in the world. As a businesswoman and community leader, she has the keen ability to recognize how decisions and actions affect the big picture. While she could probably write volumes about what it takes to be business savvy — with expert marketing, leadership skills, and going all in — the book Stacy says she would write would be about the importance of kindness and connection.

Stacy shared with me a visual of how she wished we could all see the world. Imagine if you were able to hover above the world and see the web that connects each one of us. If we were able to clearly see our connection with one another, we would see how a simple act of kindness has a profound ripple effect. Like casting a pebble into a lake, an act of kindness not only affects the person who is the recipient but affects the next person the recipient interacts with, and the next. Keeping the bird's eye visual of our web of connection in mind, suddenly kindness takes on an entirely new power.

We didn't discuss detailed specifics of what shape her book would take. Perhaps it would contain testimonials of how someone's kind act changed a day, a moment, or a life — woven with ideas from Stacy's own life of leadership and philanthropy. I'm sure she would urge leaders in the community to step up and add a little more *kindness* to their daily practice. She would remind her readers that the CEO is just as connected to the janitor as to the vice-president of the company.

While she has not yet written a book, I can see Stacy's story being shared through the way she moves through her life. She actively sets an intention to live life with kindness. Her intention includes one of her legacies, The Opportunities for Success Scholarship Program, which she co-founded. The scholarship provides college education scholarships for low-income women, giving them the opportunity to reach their greatest potential through education. Just as with all acts of kindness, each scholarship granted not only touches the recipient's life, but also impacts the recipient's family and community. While it is nearly impossible to track the far-reaching effect that a college degree can have on families and on the generations that follow, or on the recipients' communities and the people they may end up serving, it is heartwarming to imagine the long-lasting results.

In addition to testimonials interwoven throughout the book, I also imagine that Stacy's book would include chapters covering nuts and bolts — practical steps on how to give back to one's community. She and I reside in the same area of Washington state, where I've seen her name appear on several non-profit endeavors. I wonder if Stacy has ever compiled a complete list of all the non-profit events she has either co-chaired or advised. She doesn't simply lend her name to an event; she rolls up her sleeves and puts her heart and soul into helping causes she believes in to reach their goals. Perhaps the book would help leaders identify which causes align with their personal mission statements. She would surely urge her readers to form partnerships with the communities where they do business.

As our conversation continued, I found myself feeling excited about the substantial impact a book written by Stacy — sharing her views on kindness, connection, and leadership — would have.

Towards the end of our time together, Stacy mentioned one of her favorite quotes by American poet, memoirist, and Civil Rights activist Maya Angelou: "I've learned that people will forget what you said, people will forget what you did, but people will never forget how you made them feel."

Sitting with Stacy and having this conversation was a testament to this quote. I left my time with Stacy that afternoon feeling connected to the people around me and wrapped in a blanket of kindness.

# Journal

*Today's date is:*

-------------------------------------------------------------

*Journal prompt: If you had to write a book, what would you write about?*

-------------------------------------------------------------

-------------------------------------------------------------

-------------------------------------------------------------

-------------------------------------------------------------

-------------------------------------------------------------

-------------------------------------------------------------

-------------------------------------------------------------

-------------------------------------------------------------

-------------------------------------------------------------

-------------------------------------------------------------

-------------------------------------------------------------

-------------------------------------------------------------

-------------------------------------------------------------

-------------------------------------------------------------

# *Ask Yourself This*

## Inspiration and Motivation:
## Shari's Own Reflections

1.  *What's your favorite quotation?* "If today were the last day of your life, would you be doing what you are doing now?" This anonymous quote is my beacon. I think about it several times during any given day. It comes in handy when I'm feeling angst or anger — feelings I don't want to waste my precious time on while I am here on Earth. Thinking about this quote gives me the pause I need to take a step back from any situation so that I can see the many opportunities and choices available to me.

2.  *What lessons did you learn this past year, and how have you grown and improved?* This past year I learned to trust my gut, my intuition, what I feel. Intuition is a sense that we all possess; but being able to tap into our intuition is a skill that we can lose if we let the fear of judgment and insecurity creep in. With the intentional practice of listening to my gut, my level of angst dissipates because I can proceed confidently with actions that align with my true desire.

Trusting my intuition has also allowed me to be a wiser guide for others in my work as a life coach. I have noticed that through the practice of trusting my intuition in my own life, I have been able to listen not only with my ears to my clients, but also with my intuitive nature. This allows me to tap into what is going on below the surface for my clients, to ask the questions that best assist them in bringing out their truths. Learning to trust my intuition this past year has made me a much more effective life coach and leader.

3. *How are you creating a life well lived?* I have let go of the fear of judgment, which has allowed me to live freely to pursue my passion — of writing, coaching, relationship-building, and community — all while giving myself the grace to make mistakes, learn, and grow along the way. I am truly living my life to the fullest. I believe that I am making a positive impact on the world, one relationship at a time.

4. *What song best describes your life?* My favorite two songs are *Beyond* by Leon Bridges and *You and I* by John Legend. I think these two songs describe the way I want to feel: I am enough, and I am beautiful just the way I am. These tunes are so much more fitting than the song I used to play on my way to work when I was in my 20s, *I Will Survive* by Gloria Gaynor. While I still love the song and sing along whenever I hear it, I am certainly glad it is no longer the song I need to listen to every morning to get through my workday!

5. *If you had to write a book, what would you write about?* My girlfriends! Well, that was an easy answer for me. Moving forward, I am going to travel across the United States next year, meeting one woman in each of our fifty states for coffee. I want to find out what brought her to her city and state, to learn about the community she has created, to find out what her definition of friendship is, and to learn about her views on aging.

   While I'm not necessarily curious about what her political and religious beliefs are, I am interested in learning whether she believes the same as her parents; and if not, then when that changed for her. I look forward to writing about this incredible experience which will take an entire year to complete. I expect it will not only be memorialized in my next book, but it will also change my life for the better.

# Ask Yourself This

Beyond Today

# Day 47

## If you found out you were going to die in a year, how would you spend the next 365 days?

Karyn
Born: Tacoma, Washington
Headstone: Grateful for a wonderful life

K aryn and I met nearly a decade ago at SeaTac airport, just before boarding a plane for a girls' trip to Las Vegas. As I look back at the women who made up our group of six, it was an interesting combination — many of us meeting for the first time. It turned out to be a fun weekend filled with a lot of laughter, good food, sun, and great conversations. In fact, any stranger who observed our group over that weekend would have assumed that all of us had been friends for years.

*Day 47: If you found out you were going to die in a year, how would you spend the next 365 days?*

Karyn and I reside over an hour's drive from each other, so we chose to meet over Zoom for this conversation. Even through Zoom, the emotions brought up by this question were clearly visible. I asked Karyn if she thinks much about dying. She admitted that since she has moved into her 50s, mortality crosses her mind more than it had in past decades. Death was something she used to fear, until her dad died. Now it doesn't seem as scary to her.

Karyn didn't go through a bucket list of items that she would hope to check off if she found that she had just a year to live. Instead, she said that her immediate focus would be on spending time with her family, making sure they felt comfort and closure. Karyn has been married for nearly twenty-five years, and she has four adult children — her youngest, her only daughter, was nineteen years old at the time of our Zoom date.

Family has always been Karyn's focus in life. She chose to stay home with her kids, happily being the "mom taxi" for over two decades — to school, extracurricular activities, and weekends filled with every type of sport, especially baseball. This past year, as a relatively new empty-nester, she decided to help her husband by working in the store of the family's farm, Sterino Farms (www. sterinofarms.com). While she enjoys interacting with customers, her real joy comes from knowing that she has been able to help ease some of the burden her husband was carrying.

Karyn's dad battled brain cancer for several years — dying from the devastating disease five years ago. Karyn was very close to him, so his death was incredibly painful. One silver lining throughout his battle with cancer was that he and her mom lived nearby. Karyn was able to visit him often during his illness, taking the kids with her during many of her visits, which always cheered him up. While she very much appreciates the gift of time she had with her dad, which allowed her time to prepare as much as she could for his death, she regrets that during her many visits, they never talked about the elephant in the room: She never asked him about his experience with dying.

She wonders now what her dad's thoughts were and what conversations they could have had. She can't help but think that talking to him about his experience would have helped her feel some closure when he died. She wonders if having those conversations would have made losing him just a little less painful.

Given the pain she experienced following her dad's death along with the regret she feels for missing the opportunity for intimate conversations, she says that if she knew she were going to die and had a year to prepare, she would spend that year with her family and other loved ones. And, during that year, she would have those difficult conversations about dying.

Ideally, she would carve out time to take a little vacation with each of her children separately, followed by time away with her husband; then she would take time away with a close group of friends. She describes her friendship circle as small and very meaningful. She would take time to let individuals know what they mean to her, and she would also invite questions. She especially would encourage questions from her children. She would want her kids to experience the closure that she was not able to experience with her dad.

Karyn emphasized that if you are given the gift of extra time to know when death is imminent, then having important discussions about death — sharing feelings and questions surrounding loss — is important. Otherwise, the gift of time would be wasted, and the death would be no different from a sudden loss.

At some point, we all have just 365 days to live. Most of us don't know when that clock will start ticking. We need to let go of the fear of talking about death and have those conversations with the people we love, carving out that special time together now.

# Journal

*Today's date is:*

------------------------------------------------

*Journal prompt: If you found out you were going to die in a year, how would you spend the next 365 days?*

------------------------------------------------

------------------------------------------------

------------------------------------------------

------------------------------------------------

------------------------------------------------

------------------------------------------------

------------------------------------------------

------------------------------------------------

------------------------------------------------

------------------------------------------------

------------------------------------------------

------------------------------------------------

------------------------------------------------

------------------------------------------------

------------------------------------------------

------------------------------------------------

# Day 48

## Have you ever had an experience that led you to believe in angels or ghosts?

Natalie
Born: Seattle
Headstone: Mother. Wife. Entrepreneur. Friend.

I feel as if I've known Natalie much longer than the six years we've been friends. We initially met when I booked a photo session at her studio. Natalie specializes in photographing women (www. nataliewallacephotography.com). She brings their inner beauty out in a session that rivals a high-end professional fashion magazine shoot. Her photo shoots include professional hair and make-up with the option of professional wardrobe styling. From the moment a client walks into the studio she feels not only pampered but also *seen*. For many women, being photographed by Natalie is a life-changing experience. It is not unusual for her clients to experience a renewed feeling of confidence, focusing for the first time in years on their inner and outer beauty and sexuality — which had been neglected during years of focusing on work and child-rearing.

*Day 48: Have you ever had an experience that led you to believe in angels or ghosts?*

The second time Natalie and I worked together was on a project that was designed as a team competition for a local non-profit. Our team was comprised of ten dynamic women. I was one of the two co-chairs of our team, and Natalie was our team's photographer and videographer. While the competition had some issues beyond our control, which made the experience a challenge, working together through the difficulties proved in the end to be an unforgettable bonding experience — and the first of many projects and adventures together.

It was during the time of our non-profit project that I received a devastating diagnosis: breast cancer. My immediate response was to believe that this diagnosis was given to me as an opportunity to grow and to become a better person. I tried to remain positive. But as any woman newly diagnosed, I feared what the treatment would do to my body, to my appearance. I quickly decided that the best course of action was to proceed with a double mastectomy. It was unknown until after the surgery whether radiation and chemotherapy would be part of my treatment; however, with a double mastectomy — as opposed to a lumpectomy — the chance of having to turn to radiation and chemotherapy was greatly reduced.

I wanted to capture myself before surgery and before treatment — I wanted to capture my *before-cancer self*. I contacted Natalie and she agreed to photograph me. She gave me the opportunity to shoot what I deemed my *f#ck cancer* photo shoot. Natalie gave me the photo shoot as a gift, and the whole experience lifted my spirits. It was my day to take control — to "yell" at cancer through Natalie's lens.

Then, just a couple of years later, we ventured out to our next project, the photo shoot for the interior of my debut book, *The 50/50 Friendship Flow: Life Lessons From And For My Girlfriends*. For this book, I needed photographs of over forty women. When I approached Natalie with this ambitious project, she was game. She opened her studio, and over the course of three very full days, she shot the amazing women who were the subjects of the book.

Following the book's photo shoot, I had the opportunity to work with Natalie two more times — once for my own social-media branding, and the other for a project for Natalie which she called *Fifty Over Fifty*. In this project, she shot fifty women who were over the age of fifty, showcasing their beauty. A few months after my momentous fiftieth birthday, I was honored to be one of her celebrated subjects.

Then came my second book, *Make Your Mess Your Message*, which was due to my publisher in early 2021, during the covid-19 pandemic. Vaccines were beginning to roll out at the time of the photo shoot, but it was a slow roll-out, done in phases across the country. Most of the women in the book had not yet been vaccinated. The social-distancing requirements meant that we couldn't bring the fifty-one women who were the subjects of the book into Natalie's studio.

In the spirit of the book, we took our mess and made it our message. Over a period of two days, Natalie shot all fifty-one women from my living room couch, via Zoom, through my large smart TV. It was certainly messy — with different challenges regarding lighting, background, screen glare, and so on. She was shooting not only through my television screen but also had to deal with the phone or computer screen from which each woman was shooting. We laughed and had a great time through the whole mess! We had the grace of black-and-white, which helped make the photos appear as uniform as possible. Overall, the photos turned out better than we expected.

A few times while chatting during shoots, Natalie shared stories of her divine connection with the spirit world. She has shared unique experiences with me, experiences that she rarely shares in casual conversation. While she is becoming more comfortable sharing her experiences, she has been quite cautious in the past — especially when she was younger, because she was afraid of appearing weird to others, afraid of judgment. But as she has grown older, she has learned to embrace her experiences as simply a part of who she is.

Natalie's mom is native Aleut, from the Aleutian Islands in the Bering Sea. Both her mother and grandmother have similar connections to the spirit world. Throughout her childhood, a connection with the spirit world was simply a part of everyday life. I could listen all day to story after story of Natalie's experiences.

For brevity's sake, I'll share just a couple of her amazing experiences — ones that have made an impression on me. Natalie vividly recalls a day from her childhood when she was with her mom at her grandmother's house. While everyone, including Natalie, was seated in the front living room area of her grandmother's home, the front door suddenly swung open with a gust of wind. Shortly after the door opened, a noise was heard from her grandmother's kitchen. It sounded as if someone was in there. One of the adults ventured into the kitchen to investigate the sound, and found that a teacup had been pulled from a high cabinet shelf and placed on the counter. Natalie's family would soon learn that Natalie's great-grandmother had died at about the same moment in time that the incident occurred. Her great-grandmother was a tea drinker!

Another story that Natalie shared with me was an experience that she had while on her way home from attending the funeral of her co-worker's baby. The baby had been born with a heart deformity and didn't survive the open-heart surgery that was performed. Natalie cried throughout the day. With a young son herself, the thought of burying a child was disturbing. As she drove towards home, she glanced back in her rearview mirror. Although she was alone in the car, she saw a being sitting in the back seat of her vehicle. She immediately locked eyes with the being. As she tells it, she has no doubt that she was seeing one of her guardian angels. When this happened, she immediately felt a sense of utter calm envelope her. As Natalie shared this story, I, too, could feel the peace she described. It was as if the retelling of the experience brought that same tranquility back, making itself present again.

While most of Natalie's experiences with the spirit world have been positive, she has had more than one frightening experience. One of her more alarming experiences happened during a time when she and a colleague were planning to produce a documentary about the supernatural. During their research, she had an encounter with what appeared to be a demented soul. While finishing up a few work items late one evening from her bedroom, with her computer open, she saw a creature crawling on the floor of her hallway. The production was halted due to the increased paranormal activity that started to occur. I am hesitant to write much about that experience because I get goosebumps just thinking about it.

Based on her life experiences and her Native culture, Natalie firmly believes that there is a battle between good and evil — and that we are constantly being pulled in both directions. It is our place here in this life to learn and grow. Natalie's mystical encounters have helped her better understand life. She understands that when things happen, whether they are positive or negative, a grand plan is in place. This understanding allows her to move through life's problems with a healthy perspective, even in the most challenging of times.

Natalie has used her gifts in her photography. She can truly and fully see her clients. She sees their spirit, their inner beauty, which helps her to bring out their true radiance.

Natalie reminds me that our day-to-day problems are presented to us as opportunities for us to learn and grow. She reminds me that there is a much greater plan. We can trust life's journey.

# Journal

*Today's date is:*

---

*Journal prompt: Have you ever had an experience that has led you to believe in angels or ghosts?*

---

---

---

---

---

---

---

---

---

---

---

---

---

---

---

# Day 49

# When did a guardian angel show up in your life?

Mandy
Born: Lake City, Minnesota
Front of Headstone: Until we meet again
Back of Headstone: Returned to sender

I met Mandy about seven years ago. My girlfriend invited me to a shopping event at her home featuring Mandy Moon Jewelry (www.mandymoonjewelry.com). Because of that event, I not only met a beautiful friend, but I have also garnered a collection of the most marvelous fashionable bracelets and necklaces.

*Day 49: When did a guardian angel show up in your life?*

Mandy is very close to her mom. In fact, her mother moved to Washington state from Minnesota to be close to Mandy. At the time of our meeting, even though I had met Mandy's mom only in passing, each time I witnessed her interacting with Mandy, I longed to have that close and loving relationship with my own mom.

Unfortunately, Mandy's relationship with her dad was quite different from the close bond she shares with her mom. He was an alcoholic who, by Mandy's teenage years, was for all practical purposes absent from her life. He let her down so many times, that she stopped trying to create the father-daughter relationship that she yearned for. To protect herself from further hurt, she distanced herself from him, rarely seeing him as she entered adulthood. It appeared that he had chosen his addiction over his relationships with his children — a painful realization for any daughter or son to have.

As adults, Mandy's brother maintained more contact with their dad. When their father was dying of cancer, he let her know that if she wanted to see him, she didn't have the luxury of time to wait. Prior to her visit, she wrote her dad a letter, pouring out all the feelings of disappointment and pain from childhood. In this way, she wanted to release any negative and painful feelings before seeing him in person. She didn't want what she knew would more than likely be the final time spent with him to be filled with bitterness. Her visit with him turned out to be the best visit she ever had with him. He died two weeks later.

In 2011, shortly after her father passed away, Mandy attended a concert at a state fair with a girlfriend. Her friend is someone known as a medium, but not one who uses her gifts to make a living.

Mandy and her friend were having fun at the fair, enjoying rides before the concert, when seemingly out of the blue, her friend stopped and said something to the effect of, "Okay, this guy is really starting to bug me. He's been hanging around you all evening." She went on to describe the man she saw next to Mandy — and the description fit her dad exactly. Her friend, who seemed slightly annoyed, said that the man kept poking her in the arm with his finger, insisting on getting her attention — something that Mandy's dad had often done in conversation! Her friend looked Mandy in the eye and said very matter-of-factly, "He wants me to tell you that he wasn't there for you then, but he's here for you now."

Mandy was stunned, but her friend then turned and went on as if nothing out of the ordinary had happened. It took Mandy awhile to allow what she had just heard to sink in.

Since that day at the fair, whenever Mandy feels worry creep in — like when her eldest son is on the football field and she worries for his safety — she thinks about her dad. With her thoughts, she reminds him that he promised to be with her and take care of her. Calling upon him gives her a sense of calm. She feels his presence and experiences a calmness, believing that he is on the field taking care of her son.

Mandy's experience with her father is not the only experience that has led her to believe in guardian angels. She was raised close to her maternal grandmother, who passed away years ago. About five years ago, when she was feeling overwhelmed, alone lying on her bed, she felt someone grab her arm — and it shocked her. She immediately sensed her grandmother's voice, telling her that she would be okay. The feelings of being overwhelmed drifted away, and she realized she really would be okay. The squeeze on her arm had been exactly the way her grandma would grab people as she spoke to them.

Without a doubt, Mandy knows she has these two guardian angels.

A number that Mandy sees regularly is 11:11. While going through her day, she'll often look down at her watch, and it will be 11:11, or she'll glance up at the clock on the microwave right at 11:11. The number appears randomly to her in other places, too. Every time she sees 11:11 she says a little prayer for her dad and grandma, a short mantra, and makes a wish. And she has manifested much of what she has wished for.

I have a similar experience of seeing a number repeatedly. Since my own dad died, I often look at my watch or clock and see 4:44. After speaking with Mandy, I've started to say a little prayer, a small mantra, and I make a wish each time I see that number. It makes me smile and puts a little extra moment of serenity into my day.

Talking to Mandy reminds me that not only can we still have a relationship with our loved ones after they pass; but also, that it is never too late to build, enrich, and heal a relationship.

# Journal

*Today's date is:*

---

*Journal prompt: When did a guardian angel show up in your life?*

---

---

---

---

---

---

---

---

---

---

---

---

---

---

# Day 50

## What have you learned about life from loss and death?

Cathi
Born: Salt Lake City, Utah
Headstone: Capable, creative, charismatic.
A classic force of nature.

Imet Cathi in July of 2021, celebrating my neighbor's birthday at a brunch I hosted. During 2021, when large gatherings were cautioned against due to the pandemic, I decided to host monthly birthday brunches for girlfriends. If I had room at the table, I would invite each birthday guest to bring a friend. Cathi was my neighbor's special guest.

*Day 50: What have you learned about life from loss and death?*

While I never met Cathi's late husband, Ken, I felt that I got to know the best part of him from my conversation with her. He was incredibly kind and loving to everyone he met. He was unforgettable. He passed away suddenly four years ago due to a blood clot in one of his lungs. Cathi wasn't prepared to lose him.

In the years since he has been gone, Cathi has learned about life from loss, as she has been forced to carve out a new identity for herself as a single woman.

Cathi focused on two areas of what she has learned about life from the loss and death of her beloved husband. One is how much she missed having his constant cheerleading spirit. She always knew that he was her number-one fan and loved her to the core; she just didn't realize how much she would miss that constant showing of love and support. Cathi was his dream girl, and he never let her forget how proud he was of her and how proud he was to have her on his arm. During their twenty-two years of marriage, he told her time and time again that she was the most beautiful woman in the world. He made her a latte each morning, and if he knew that she wanted a light breakfast — whether it was a bowl of blueberries, a breakfast bar, or simply making sure her vitamins were ready for her — he happily prepared these things to begin her day. He loved letting her know how special she was to him. It was the little things he did constantly that showed her how much he loved her. He put her on a pedestal, making her feel like the most important person in the world.

Cathi appreciated her husband during their life together, and she always knew their union was special; but she didn't realize how deep the loss of her constant cheerleader would feel.

The second learning point that Cathi focused on during our discussion was her own growth and independence. From the time she was a teen, Cathi had always been a part of a couple. She'd always had someone by her side. After her husband's death, she found strength in her independence. She laughed when she shared with me that it even came down to learning how to make her own lattes each morning. When she found that it was impossible for her to use the complicated machine her husband had used, she simplified the process with a capsule coffeemaker. She learned that she was okay going to events on her own. She learned to trust herself.

Cathi has found that no matter what comes her way, she has the strength, resources, and ability to figure it out. For the first time in her life, she sees how strong she really is, and she knows with certainty that she can get through anything and accomplish anything.

Cathi reminds me that even from our greatest losses, some of our best growth can happen. Right now, I'm in the newly empty-nester phase of life. I imagine the next stage for me and for many of my peers will be that our kids will get married, we will become grandparents, and then there will be the loss of a partner.

While not everyone experiences life in that order, looking at life's journey and thinking about what is ahead makes my conversation with Cathi more meaningful. I find comfort in her experience. No matter what life has in store for each of us, there is love, grace, and learning that can occur at every turn.

# Journal

*Today's date is:*

-------------------------------------------------------

*Journal prompt: What have you learned about life from loss and death?*

-------------------------------------------------------

-------------------------------------------------------

-------------------------------------------------------

-------------------------------------------------------

-------------------------------------------------------

-------------------------------------------------------

-------------------------------------------------------

-------------------------------------------------------

-------------------------------------------------------

-------------------------------------------------------

-------------------------------------------------------

-------------------------------------------------------

-------------------------------------------------------

-------------------------------------------------------

-------------------------------------------------------

"If today were the last day of your life, would you be doing what you are doing now?"
— Anonymous

# Day 51

## What would you hope would be said in your eulogy?

Toni
Born: Dallas, Texas
Headstone: If you don't want the truth then don't ask
the question

Toni lives three houses away from me in our quiet single-street neighborhood. For being such a small neighborhood, made up of just sixteen homes, our neighbors keep to themselves, with not much more than a polite hello or a wave shared as we pass one another. But Toni is the exception. She, like me, is very social. She has a large circle of friends from all backgrounds. So, I think it was our similar outgoing nature that sparked our friendship.

*Day 51: What would you hope would be said in your eulogy?*

I love this question. I used it as a starting point to draft my own personal mission statement. When I shared this question with Toni, after giving it some serious thought, she shared with me what she hopes would be said by her friends and family. While both groups are very important to Toni, her two children — now age thirty-six and forty-one — have always been the most important people in her life. While her husband is also a constant source of love and support, she was a single mom for fourteen years. Her children were her priority as she proudly raised them to be the fine adults they are now. She has many reasons to feel happy about the adults they've become, but what she is most proud of is that they are kind. Each is unique, very different from the other, but both move through the world with confidence and kindness, treating people they meet with respect and dignity.

My ears perked up as Toni told me about the adults her children have become. I am proud to say that my two children — who are now twenty-two and twenty — are similarly kind young adults. Hoping that my children continue on their positive path, I wanted to know what was most important to her as she raised her children.

While incredibly close to both her children, it has always been important to Toni that she is their *parent*, not their *friend*. There is a special, distinctive relationship between a parent and a child. She loves her children unconditionally. One thing that she hopes her children will say during her eulogy is that she was always fair — that she recognized their individual strengths and talents, and that she was impartial in the way she supported, disciplined, and showed her love. Her children have adopted her commitment to the importance of ethics and fairness, acknowledging that everyone has strengths and weaknesses regardless of their differences in appearance, income level, or beliefs.

As mentioned earlier, Toni's life is not just rich with family, but also with meaningful friendships. If you were to view Toni's circle of friends you'd find a lot of diversity — not simply ethnic diversity, but also economic, age, political, and religious differences. As a teenager, Toni's parents sent her to an all-girls' boarding school. She credits the experience of living with her classmates as the catalyst for gaining the understanding that people are much more than their outward appearance. Living with her classmates at a young age taught her that everyone has a story and a family life — which may turn out to be different from a first impression. Boarding school also showed her that we're all connected, and we all have singular strengths and challenges. She appreciates the importance of getting to really know someone.

She told one of her friends and her daughter a little bit about my project. When she mentioned that I'd asked her for a quote for her hypothetical headstone, and she shared the quote that she chose, her friend and daughter both had the same reaction: They immediately laughed, exclaiming that it was perfect! Toni is the friend that everyone can go to for an honest opinion and sound advice. She values integrity and reliability. When she gives an opinion, she gives it knowing that the receiver deserves the respect of honesty, even when it may sting a little.

Fortunately, she's also a gifted communicator. She shares her opinions, but she also remains open to dialogue. She helps people through any hard decisions they have to make — she's an ear for friends, family, and clients. Accountability, trust, and forgiveness come naturally for Toni. She doesn't expect anyone to be perfect; but she does expect others — and herself — to own up to mistakes.

In the end, she hopes that in her eulogy her values will be remembered — because that will mean that she has lived them, and that they were felt by the people she loved: "She was a fair and loyal mother, wife, and friend — a woman who always strived to do what is right, even though sometimes that meant the path was a harder one to travel."

# Journal

*Today's date is:*

---------------------------------------------------------------

*Journal prompt: What would you hope would be said in your eulogy?*

---------------------------------------------------------------

---------------------------------------------------------------

---------------------------------------------------------------

---------------------------------------------------------------

---------------------------------------------------------------

---------------------------------------------------------------

---------------------------------------------------------------

---------------------------------------------------------------

---------------------------------------------------------------

---------------------------------------------------------------

---------------------------------------------------------------

---------------------------------------------------------------

---------------------------------------------------------------

---------------------------------------------------------------

# *Ask Yourself This*

# Beyond Today:
# Shari's Own Reflections

1. *If you found out you were going to die in a year, how would you spend the next 365 days?* I would write about my experience and ask someone I trust to publish my writings after I die. I would spend as much time as I could with my immediate family. I would throw a going-away party for myself — a huge party with over 500 people in attendance — with the most heartwarming, humorous, and tear-jerking speech that I could create. I would try to make a positive impact on as many lives as I could during the year I had left. Honestly, I would not change much of what I'm doing now. I currently live as if I were dying. I make the most of every day and I don't believe in wasting a single day.

2. *Have you ever had an experience that led you to believe in angels or ghosts?* I have not had such an experience, but nevertheless I do believe in the supernatural — including angels and ghosts. When I was a child, I was very fearful of the supernatural. I think

in part my fear stemmed from the way religious beliefs were taught to me. As an adult, I find comfort in believing that there is an unseen world — that life doesn't end when our human bodies die.

Ever since my dad died, I see the number 444 everywhere. I'll glance at the clock, and it will read 4:44. I always feel at peace and loved when I see those numbers appear. Of course, seeing 444 is not an angel or a ghost sighting. And perhaps I'm simply seeing repeating numbers because I like the fact that it gives me comfort. Regardless of the reason, the feelings of serenity and love are always welcome.

3.   *When did a guardian angel show up in your life?* A month after my twenty-second birthday, I was involved in a horrific head-on car accident that sent me to our region's level-one trauma hospital. Both of my legs were broken; my right ankle was crushed; my eyelids were sliced off by the front windshield glass; my left cheek was gouged from contact with the shattering glass on the driver's-side window; and I had additional deep lacerations covering my face.

I've already shared my experience with the stranger who came on the scene to help comfort me until the first responders arrived (see my answer from Day 26); but I also had a second guardian angel. On one very difficult day in the hospital, I was depressed and crying non-stop, lying helpless in my hospital bed, when the night janitor stopped to talk to me. He told me I would be okay. He said it in a way that instantly made me feel loved. I suddenly felt calm, somehow genuinely knowing I really would be okay. That janitor was an older immigrant with a thick accent, and it is his face and voice that I instantly think of whenever I'm asked if a guardian angel has ever shown up in my life.

4. *What have you learned about life from loss and death?* I've learned that the only thing that can truly heal grief is time. I've learned that memories of a loved one never fade — they just become less painful to remember. I've learned that life is short, so be purposeful each day — because each day is a gift. I've learned to tell people now what they mean to me, instead of waiting to make a speech at their memorial service. I've learned that you can have a relationship with someone even after they die, because you can connect on an energetic spiritual level; and even that relationship can change and grow over time.

5. *What would you hope would be said in your eulogy?* "Shari made the world a better place by having an impact on every person she met along the way."

# Ask Yourself This

Complete The
#60dayjournalchallenge

# Journal Prompts

## Journal days 52–60

Remember at the beginning of the book I told you that it takes roughly sixty days to form a habit? If you have been following along, you're now ready for day fifty-two — just nine days to go towards that sixty-day mark. The next nine days come with simple journal prompts, without stories from my girlfriends. The next nine days are designed for you to decide what your next steps are in your own journaling practice. Will you create a gratitude journal, a career-change journal, a relationship journal, or a mix of all the above? Don't forget to buy a notebook to continue your own journal on day sixty-one. Or pick up the other two books in the *Friendship* series, and journal through those books, which will give you an additional 101 days of journaling with me. You can also sign up for our newsletter at www.animperfectlyperfectlife. com and receive additional self-coaching tips throughout the year!

# Day 52

Today's date is:

_____

Journal prompt: *What is the fear that has been holding you back?*

_____

_____

_____

_____

_____

_____

_____

_____

_____

_____

_____

_____

_____

_____

# Day 53

*Today's date is:*

_____

*Journal prompt: What is it about aging that scares you?*

_____

_____

_____

_____

_____

_____

_____

_____

_____

_____

_____

_____

_____

_____

_____

# Day 54

Today's date is:

_____

Journal prompt: What in your relationship with your partner/child/ friend/co-worker needs healing?

_____

_____

_____

_____

_____

_____

_____

_____

_____

_____

_____

_____

_____

_____

_____

# Day 55

*Today's date is:*

------------------------------------------------------------

*Journal prompt: What do you view as your top three natural talents?*

------------------------------------------------------------

------------------------------------------------------------

------------------------------------------------------------

------------------------------------------------------------

------------------------------------------------------------

------------------------------------------------------------

------------------------------------------------------------

------------------------------------------------------------

------------------------------------------------------------

------------------------------------------------------------

------------------------------------------------------------

------------------------------------------------------------

------------------------------------------------------------

------------------------------------------------------------

# Day 56

*Today's date is:*

-------------------------------------------------------------------

*Journal prompt: Who are the people (including yourself) in your life that you love unconditionally? Describe what unconditional love means to you.*

-------------------------------------------------------------------

-------------------------------------------------------------------

-------------------------------------------------------------------

-------------------------------------------------------------------

-------------------------------------------------------------------

-------------------------------------------------------------------

-------------------------------------------------------------------

-------------------------------------------------------------------

-------------------------------------------------------------------

-------------------------------------------------------------------

-------------------------------------------------------------------

-------------------------------------------------------------------

-------------------------------------------------------------------

-------------------------------------------------------------------

-------------------------------------------------------------------

# Day 57

*Today's date is:*

------------------------------------------------------------

*Journal prompt: What has been your biggest mistake and what have you learned from it?*

------------------------------------------------------------

------------------------------------------------------------

------------------------------------------------------------

------------------------------------------------------------

------------------------------------------------------------

------------------------------------------------------------

------------------------------------------------------------

------------------------------------------------------------

------------------------------------------------------------

------------------------------------------------------------

------------------------------------------------------------

------------------------------------------------------------

------------------------------------------------------------

------------------------------------------------------------

# Day 58

Today's date is:

---

Journal prompt: What can you promise to do tomorrow to make it even greater than today?

---

---

---

---

---

---

---

---

---

---

---

---

---

---

# Day 59

*Today's date is:*

------------------------------------------------------------

*Journal prompt: What do you want written on your headstone?*

------------------------------------------------------------

------------------------------------------------------------

------------------------------------------------------------

------------------------------------------------------------

------------------------------------------------------------

------------------------------------------------------------

------------------------------------------------------------

------------------------------------------------------------

------------------------------------------------------------

------------------------------------------------------------

------------------------------------------------------------

------------------------------------------------------------

------------------------------------------------------------

------------------------------------------------------------

# Day 60

*Today's date is:*

----------------------------------------

*Journal prompt: You've now journaled for sixty days and made it a daily habit. What have you learned about yourself in the process?*

----------------------------------------

----------------------------------------

----------------------------------------

----------------------------------------

----------------------------------------

----------------------------------------

----------------------------------------

----------------------------------------

----------------------------------------

----------------------------------------

----------------------------------------

----------------------------------------

----------------------------------------

----------------------------------------

# Going Forward

The *Friendship* series, which started out as a personal endeavor, became a three-year project of love — consisting of 152 dates with 144 different women. They are diverse in age, race, ethnicity, economic background, educational background, and political and religious views. They represent so many individual characteristics, talents, and experiences — each beautifully unique. I made a connection with and learned from each and every woman. This experience has been so profound that I've spent a good part of my waking hours figuring out how to share these special dates with you.

I would love to connect with you, my readers, who have followed this journey alongside me. Please let me know how this book and your journaling practice has impacted your life.

If you haven't already, you can continue journaling through the *Friendship* series, by going back to read the first two books, which also include journal prompts. Share the series with a girlfriend or your book club — and journal and grow together!

My passion is coaching women who are in their fabulous yet tricky middle years of life. I invite you to learn more by going to my website www.animperfectlyperfectlife.com.

# Acknowledgments

This book is the final of the *Friendship* series — thank you to the women who are the series stars: CC, Elyse, Kayley, Dede, Martha, Vanessa, Lizzy, Jen C., Diane, Tori, Barb, Michelle F., Michelle N., Imelda, Shelley, Michelle T., Mim, Erin, Kathy, Suzanne, Tracey, Laverne, Dana F., Celia, Natalie, Cindy W., Tanya, Tee-Ta, Alanda, Carey, Mary, Lisa, Tammy, Rachel, Meredith, Chanel, Sonya, Sarah G., Susie, Renee, Yolanda B., Lexi, Linda, Rosa, Amber, Belinda, Kate, Cindy B., Bernadette, Michele, Sarah N., Tina, Kelli, Angie, Tawan, Leah, Alla, Jen J., Sarah E., Paige, Jane, Jiawen, Melissa, Caron, Jen H., Kathryn K., Gage, Sarah R., Susan, Rose, Maja, Shay, Mari, Alex, Teri, Cati, Lilla, Shalonda, Carrie, Dee, Carolyn, Bunni, Sarah M., Cindy P., Lennaea, Tracy, Ronda, Yolanda S., Roxanne, Stacey Z., Angela E., Tracie, Kirsten, Theresa, Simone, Tiffani, Connie, Julie, Michelle P., Angela S., Sabrina, Arlene, Melissa C., Mayumi, Kim, Karen Z., Patti, Christine, Stacey C., Cindy J., Justina, LaShanda, Lori, Denise, Angela J., Veronica, Sarah P., Sadie, Nancy, Vivian, Sheila, Stephanie, Trina, Rebecca, Heidi, Lyanne, Michelle S., Nicole, Kathryn R., Christi, Athina, Trish, Deci, Karen P., Anne Marie, Dana L., Kimberly, Janel, Alane, Stacy L., Karyn, Natalie, Mandy, Cathi, and Toni.

In addition to my girlfriends, I would also like to thank the women I've met along this journey: my virtual assistant Carissa Ang; my publisher Christine Kloser and her team of amazing women including Carrie, Karen, and Jean; my media trainer, Paula Rizzo; my publicist, Kourtney Jason and her team including digital marketing professional Rebecca; my editor Janis; my professional website designer Kristin Prius; photographers Natalie Wallace and Wendy K. Yalom; and make-up and hair artists Dana Tao and Rickie Bocanegra.

Finally, I thank my family — Rory, Alexis, and Zachary — who consistently support and love me unconditionally. My family includes our active yellow lab, Nitro, who makes sure I take breaks throughout my workday, and our new brown lab puppy, Thunder. I also write in loving memory of Boomerang, our beautiful twelve-and-a-half-year-old black lab, who we lost last year to cancer. He was the best family dog and will be forever missed.

# Contact Us

An Imperfectly Perfect Life®, LLC
PO Box 592
Redmond, WA 98073

www.animperfectlyperfectlife.com

Let's get social:

Facebook www.facebook.com/animperfectlyperfectlife
Instagram www.instagram.com/an_imperfectly_perfect_life/
LinkedIn www.linkedin.com/in/shari-leid-51a53b10/
YouTube www.youtube.com/c/Sharileid
Twitter www.twitter.com/AnImperfectly
TikTok www.tiktok.com/@sharileid
Spotify https://open.spotify.com/
show/4JQxZUFMv49elu6N6gQi6F?si=4973aa336c7a4054
Apple Podcasts https://podcasts.apple.com/us/podcast/an-
imperfectly-perfect-life/id1589101147

Please visit www.animperfectlyperfectlife.com to view video interviews with the women you have just read about. Please sign up to receive our weekly newsletter, which contains exclusive offers, including discounts and freebies to help guide you towards creating your own imperfectly perfect life.